BRISTOL CHANNEL
PLEASURE STEAMERS

BRISTOL CHANNEL

PLEASURE STEAMERS

BY ROBERT WALL

DAVID & CHARLES:NEWTON ABBOT

For Matthew

0 7153 6069 8

Set in 11 on 13-point Plantin
and printed in Great Britain
by W J Holman Limited Dawlish
for David & Charles (Holdings) Limited
South Devon House Newton Abbot Devon

CONTENTS

LIST OF ILLUSTRATIONS

INTRODUCTION

Almost a century has passed since the brothers Peter and Alexander Campbell transferred their steamer business from the Clyde to the Bristol Channel in the spring of 1888. In doing so, they laid the foundations of one of the most popular and successful fleets of pleasure steamers in British maritime history. The war years apart, the muddy tidal waters that separate Wales from the West Country have carried Campbell steamers ever since.

The major contributory factor to this success was the Campbell brothers' use of the 'purpose-built' saloon pleasure steamer. This was in direct contrast to the miscellany of shipping types operating in the Channel excursion business when the Campbells arrived in Bristol. Many operators used paddle tugs or elderly cross-channel packets in the trade, but it was a use for which they were not designed and they proved no match for the fast comfortable saloon steamers from the Clyde.

It is now a matter of history that these saloon steamers dominated the Bristol Channel excursion trade from the very first day they arrived. Nearly all were paddle-driven, and such was their appearance and reliability that they endeared themselves to thousands of people on both sides of the estuary and far beyond. Even today, almost 20 years after her last voyage, most Bristolians over 35 recall the *Britannia*, and among enthusiasts the merits of various vessels are argued with increasing fervour (and exaggeration!) as the years go by.

This book has been compiled as a tribute to these steamers. Only steamers 'purpose-built' or ships used almost exclusively in excursion work have been included.

Because the mainstream of pleasure-steamer history in the Bristol Channel follows the fortunes of Campbell's White Funnel Fleet and its eventual triumph over all competitors, Part 1 of the book contains a brief history of this fleet. The minor fleet and private-owner histories form Part 2. Part 3 is devoted to the ships themselves.

All dimensions quoted have been taken from contemporary registers. Speeds have been taken from figures quoted by shipowners from time to time in press announcements, handbills or guide books. The author suggests, in view of past controversies, that these speeds be treated with caution!

ROBERT WALL

1 THE CAMPBELL STORY

Not far from the spot where Henry Bell started the first British commercial steamship service stands the memorial to an old Scots sailor. The northern shores of the Clyde Estuary are traditional Campbell country and it was to Kilmun on the Holy Loch that, in the late 1860s, Captain Robert Campbell came with his fleet of steamships. Captain Robert was a Clyde steamship operator of long standing, but he now concentrated on the Kilmun and Holy Loch trade, in which he was joined by his two sons, Peter and Alexander.

The 1860s saw the climax of the railway revolution, and the competition for the passenger trade on the Clyde was intense. The daily commutor traffic to the shipyards on the South Bank and to the commercial and industrial centres in Glasgow itself provided rich pickings for the successful companies, and many enterprises rose and fell as the years progressed into the 1870s. The Campbell family shared these ups and downs with the others, and were even forced to dispose of their whole fleet in the year 1884.

These commercial misfortunes led directly to the formation of the Bristol Channel company, P. & A. Campbell Ltd. Undaunted by the events of 1884, the Campbell family started their steamship line again in 1885, first buying the paddle steamer *Meg Merrilies*, 244 grt, and at the same time ordering *Waverley*, 258 grt. The Campbells put *Meg* straight back on the Glasgow to Kilmun route and achieved some success, largely due to the popularity of Captain Robert with the local inhabitants. Another steamer, *Madge Wildfire*, 220 grt, was ordered in 1886.

The spring of 1887 saw events which were to change the whole future of the Campbell family. A syndicate of Bristol businessmen, including a member of the Wills family, came north to inspect *Waverley* with a view to chartering her for work in the Bristol Channel. *Waverley* had proved something of a problem to her owners, largely because she was too big for the Glasgow-Kilmun trade, so the opportunity of chartering her to the Bristolians for the whole of the summer of 1887 was grasped with both hands. Mr Wills and his colleagues were impressed with the ship, particularly with her speed, and they engaged her to come south in May of that year. Captain Alexander Campbell, one of Captain Robert's sons, took command, and she set off from the Clyde on 19 May 1887.

During her voyage down to Bristol through the Irish Sea *Waverley* encountered some of the worst gales that stormy piece of water had experienced for years. It took her five days to do the trip, but, nevertheless, on 25 May she set off to Ilfracombe for her first excursion, and the Bristol Channel saw the Campbell house colours—a plain white funnel and a blue burgee with a white ball and chevron at the masthead—for the first time.

The arrival of *Waverley* in Bristol marked a turning point in local excursion services. In 1886, another Bristol syndicate had chartered the Clyde steamer *Bonnie Doon*, which had proved so successful that, in the winter that followed, the syndicate, headed by a Mr Nurse, had bought her outright. As a steamer, however, *Bonnie Doon* was not in the same class as the *Waverley*, and she now had to face the competition of the Campbells.

Waverley's first season at Bristol was a complete success. She proved that a fast saloon steamer, purpose-built for the job, could operate in the Channel in all weathers and provide a safe and reliable service. It was obvious that the makings of a good business were to be found in the waters that lay be-

1 *A square-rigger on her way into Bristol passes* Waverley (I) *at Hotwells pontoon. The time is probably the late 1890s*

tween Bristol and Ilfracombe in the south and Chepstow and Swansea in the north. So for the 1888 season, Captain Alec Campbell proposed to run *Waverley* as his own private venture at Bristol.

Before the 1888 season got under way, however, two events caused the Campbell family to abandon the Clyde and come south permanently. The first was the death of Captain Robert Campbell on 10 April 1888 at the age of 58. Bob Campbell was probably the most famous and certainly the most popular of the old Clyde steamboat private operators.

The Campbell brothers were nothing if not intelligent businessmen, and they could see the way that things would go. The large amounts of capital investment available to the railway companies would make them formidable opponents and very hard, if not impossible, to beat in commercial competition. Therefore, in November 1888, they sold the two steamers *Meg Merrilies* and *Madge Wildfire,* with the goodwill and all equipment on the Kilmun route, to the Caledonian Railway Company for £18,600, and came south to Bristol.

Bristol in 1887 was a changing city. The complacency and lack of enterprise which, in the early years of the nineteenth century, had allowed the maritime lead which Bristol enjoyed with London to be lost to Liverpool and other ports were gone. Active plans for the improvement of the docks were under way and the new port at Avonmouth was opened. Two years later, in 1889, a new dock opened at Portishead, just across the Avon from Avonmouth. New industries were developing, prominent among these being tobacco and cocoa. The commercial life of the city was booming. Merchants and thousands of prosperous middle-class businessmen, whose services were required by industry and the employees it attracted, began to seek new homes in the suburbs that crept out towards the villages of Westbury-on-Trym and Horfield.

To a society whose only prime movers were the railway locomotive and the horse, the novelty and adventure of an excursion by sea was a great attraction. The spotless white funnels contrasting with the acrid taste of their smoke, and the spluttering of paddle wheels churning up the muddy Avon, must have been a revelation indeed to a generation that had yet to see the aeroplane or to hear a wire-

He was so popular that many of his friends rallied round to buy the steamer *Meg Merrilies* in 1885 after he had been forced to sell his whole fleet in the previous year. His funeral became almost a triumphal procession as *Madge Wildfire* carried the coffin from the famous Broomielaw Quay in Glasgow via Greenock to Kilmun, where a service was conducted in the saloon on board, while flags of the steamers in the harbour were flown at half mast. So passed Bob Campbell, and, as if to emphasise the cold fact that the day of the private owner was passing, in the same year came the second significant event—the Caledonian Railway Company began operations at Gourock.

2 (*above*) Bonnie Doon *at Cumberland Basin, Bristol. An early opponent of the Campbells she was already operating at Bristol when* Waverley *arrived in 1887. Here she is in her original rig*

3 (*below*) Ilfracombe *in 1890. Left to right are* Lady Gwendoline (*Edwards & Robertson*), Waverley (*P. & A. Campbell*), *then the second* Lady Margaret *and* Earl of Dunraven (*both Edwards & Robertson, the latter on charter*). *Another paddler is at anchor off and there is an unidentified tug at the Stonebench*

less set. The Bristolians flocked in their hundreds and thousands to join Campbell's excursions in their first season. The future of the company was assured from the very beginning, although 1888 was a financially poor year.

Competition was not lacking, however. As already mentioned, in 1886 the Scots iron paddler *Bonnie Doon* had spent a season on charter to a Bristol syndicate that had its headquarters in the old General Draper Inn near the pier at Hotwells. *Bonnie Doon* ran in direct competition with *Waverley* in the 1887 and 1888 seasons, and in 1889 the competition was increased when the Cardiff company of Edwards & Robertson stationed its *Lady Margaret* at Bristol, with the tug *Earl of Dunraven*, which was on charter from a firm of Cardiff tug owners. A battle to the commercial death now broke out between Campbell's and Edwards & Robertson. The Welsh company added its new ship *Lady*

Gwendoline to the Bristol station in August 1889, but despite Welsh superiority in numbers, the White Funnel line always seemed to have greater local support.

This local support is interesting. At the end of the 1889 season Captain Alec Campbell had received a testimonial from a group of people described as 'season ticket holders and friends', and there is little doubt that the Bristol public already looked on the Campbell firm as its local property. Certainly the support that Campbell's got from Bristol encouraged them to build *Ravenswood*, which started operations in July 1891. This was not a moment too soon, since Edwards & Robertson produced *Lorna Doone* in June of the same year. Both ships were due to have careers of half a century or more each, and on coming into service they became the chief assets of their respective companies.

With the arrival of *Ravenswood* Captain

Peter joined his brother in Bristol to take command of *Waverley*, while Captain Alec took over the larger ship. The season was another brilliant success for the Campbells, and as *Ravenswood* tied up at Hotwells after her final run at the end of September 1891, Captain Alec was 'chaired' by an enthusiastic band of supporters, who formed an impromptu procession along the Hotwells Road.

Once again the season-ticket holders organised a testimonial for Captain Alec, and this time he collected a diamond-studded scarf ring and studs, a pair of binoculars and a Davenport writing desk, which were presented to him at a public meeting in the Royal Hotel on 22 April 1892. The meeting was notable for innumerable speeches from local worthies. From contemporary accounts, however, there emerges a clear indication of the Campbell brothers' flair for public relations. One gentleman stressed 'Captain Campbell's love of children', while another pointed out that the fleet always ran a charity trip each season on behalf of the Children's Hospital.

Alec Campbell's speech in reply is interesting. He told the gathering that in the 4 years he and his firm had operated in Bristol they had carried 250,000 passengers. He forecast that the services would soon be extended to Mumbles and Tenby. He then went on to talk about racing. Already it was common knowledge on the Channel that the rival steamships raced each other for piers. But this Captain Alec flatly denied. He blandly told his audience that it was impossible to force either *Ravenswood* or *Waverley*, and that no ships in his fleet ever took part in such dubious activities! He concluded his speech by announcing that there would be 209 commercial excursions in 1892 and a season ticket would cost two guineas.

The 1892 season proceeded with *Ravenswood* and *Waverley* running against *Lorna Doone*. The White Funnel Fleet started organising excursions in conjunction with the Midland Railway, which brought thousands of Midlanders on day trips to the Bristol Channel, and early in 1893 a further steamer was ordered. The company also went public, with a share capital of £60,000, in March of that year.

The rivalry with the Welsh company continued, and the activities of both sides seem to have exceeded normal commercial competition. It was considered fair practice to tear down the opponent's sailing bills as soon as they were posted, and when the opponent announced his sailing times, Campbell's would promptly schedule their own ship to leave 15 minutes earlier. Passengers arriving for the rival boat's sailing were then easily tempted to sail on the earlier ship. Inevitably the vessel that sailed later did its best to catch up, and a race ensued.

Charges for all this excitement are remarkable by today's standards. A trip from Bristol to Clevedon cost 1s on the foredeck and 1s 6d if you wished to make use of the saloon. By 1893 a cheap day return to Ilfracombe in the saloon cost 3s 6d.

It was on such a day return trip from Ilfracombe in the summer of 1893 that the racing between rival steamers reached a dramatic climax. In that year 5 June was a Monday, and *Ravenswood*, with Captain Alec in command, was returning from a day excursion to North Devon. She called in the evening at Lynmouth with 150 passengers, and left at the same time as *Lorna Doone*, which was carrying 250.

A race up-Channel ensued but Captain Nat Hucker of *Lorna Doone* managed to keep ahead, although Alec Campbell pressed his ship hard. As the ships drew near Steepholm, it was quite evident that one or the other would have to give way to get alongside Weston Old Pier. *Lorna Doone* held on and, as his ship was leading, Captain Hucker assumed that *Lorna Doone* would be allowed in first. However, Captain Alec maintained his course and speed and the inevitable crash resulted. *Ravenswood's* port paddle-box crashed into the side of *Lorna Doone* and passengers skidded in all directions. Evidently Captain Campbell now thought discretion the better part of valour and *Ravenswood* slowed down. *Lorna Doone* was left to hobble into Weston pier and land her passengers. She then carried on to Cardiff, while *Ravenswood* eventually returned to Bristol.

The collision took place in full view of hundreds of people, both on the steamers and at the pier head, and a Board of Trade Inquiry ensued. It opened in Bristol on 4 July and lasted for a week. In court the battle broke out afresh.

The case turned on which of the two ships was leading at the time of the accident. Both sides produced witnesses who swore that their particular champion was the leading vessel, and for good measure a lot of dirty washing was trotted out. Early in the witness box was the chief officer of *Lorna Doone*, who was adamant that *Ravenswood* was being pushed beyond her limits. 'Large flames were coming out of her funnel', he alleged. 'Nonsense', replied the Bristol people. 'No flames were coming out of the funnel—and even if they were, it was impossible to see them in daylight!' The same officer also alleged that *Ravenswood* was 'jumping out of the water' in her efforts to pass *Lorna Doone*.

Campbell's certainly fought hard to justify the conduct of *Ravenswood*. They produced a string of expert witnesses, including a Captain

Baird ('over 40 years at sea'), a Bristol Channel pilot and a captain from Plymouth. The expert evidence of these nautical gentlemen was supported by Mr Elkins of Horfield Road, Bristol, who announced that he was a member of the city council! The best that Edwards & Robertson could put up against this array of nautical and civic expertise was a Baptist minister, a jeweller and a railway guard; and the disparity of marine experience between the English and Welsh witnesses was pointed out with some glee by Captain Campbell's counsel.

When Captain Alec Campbell himself went into the witness box, the gloves really came off. The Welsh lawyers extracted from him the admission that he had once petitioned the Board of Trade in order to get Captain Hucker's certificate of competence cancelled. He admitted reluctantly that he had considered Captain Hucker unfit to hold such a certificate but the Board of Trade had turned down the petition. Worse was to follow when the Welsh side brought out that Captain Campbell's own certificate had been suspended for six months in 1891.

All this must have made an unfortunate impression on the court, and Campbell's fight to clear their captain and their ship was to no avail. The court gave its decision on 12 July 1893, and agreed with the Board of Trade solicitor, Mr Inskip, that the whole affair was 'a disgrace to the Bristol Channel'. The court found that *Ravenswood* had been 'navigated recklessly' and ordered Captain Campbell to pay £125 towards the costs of the Board of Trade. They rubbed salt into the wound by stating that in their view *Lorna Doone* had been navigated with seamanlike care, and for good measure instructed the Weston Pier Company to appoint a harbourmaster to control approaching vessels.

As the affair ended, a spokesman for P. & A. Campbell announced that they hoped the case would 'end the unfortunate rivalry between steamers' which had gone on ever since the Campbell brothers arrived in Bristol.

The court's verdict, however, was a hollow triumph for *Lorna Doone* and her Welsh owners. In the following three seasons of 1894 to 1896 the Campbell brothers added three modern steel vessels to their fleet—*Westward Ho*, *Cambria* and *Britannia*—and no commercial company can have ever made a better capital investment. The three new ships' reliability in service and their passenger acceptability made them the backbone of the company's operations for 50 years, and *Britannia* was to last until 1956. *Westward Ho* arrived in the Channel in June 1894 and was a great advance on any previous vessel; she set a standard which had to be matched by every new steamer from that time on and the use of such superior equipment put Campbell's competitors in a very difficult position. *Cambria* followed in 1895, and the bare statement that she arrived in the Bristol Channel on the evening tide of Sunday, 26 May, hides an interesting story.

She had been built by a company called McIntyre at their yard at Alloa on the Firth of Clyde and by the time *Cambria* was approaching her trials the builders were in financial difficulties. Faced with the possibility that their new steamer, on which certain progress payments had been made, would now be sold off to meet her builders' liabilities, the Campbell brothers acted in typical fashion. They travelled north with a Bristol crew, boarded *Cambria* and prepared her for sea, days ahead of the original schedule. They then took her to the Clyde and ran trials there on 24 May. Without any pause for rest, they then sailed overnight for Bristol, running down the west coast of Britain in 22 hours, calling at Penarth and Clevedon.

After finally fitting out at Underfall Yard, *Cambria* ran her first excursion on 1 June 1895 to Lynmouth and Ilfracombe direct. With Captain Alec on the bridge, it took her 3 hours 40 minutes, and fireworks and maroons were released from strategic points on the Devon coast as she passed. The whole operation was a striking example of the Campbells' determination and their appreciation of well organised publicity.

By 1896, when *Britannia* joined the fleet at a cost of £27,000, the company was fully

established and taking a large proportion of the Bristol Channel trade. In that season *Britannia* visited such places as Penzance, Falmouth and the Isles of Scilly. In the meantime, Edwards & Robertson had gone out of business at the end of 1895 and four of their ships had gone to another Cardiff owner, John Gunn. Their new vessel, *Lady Margaret*, was bought by Campbell's, and this addition

4 Britannia *leaving Hotwells pontoon, Bristol, in the late nineties. The year is probably 1897 when the pontoon was enlarged at a cost of £15,000. The work appears to be in progress*

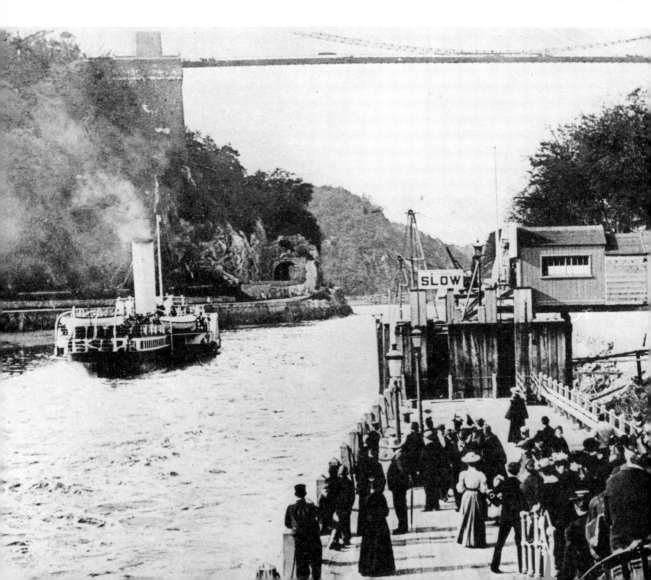

5 *L to r,* Lorna Doone, Westward Ho, Brodick Castle *and* Earl of Dunraven *at Ilfracombe in 1894. Behind are* Ravenswood *and* Brighton

brought the strength of their fleet to six. In 1896, the share capital was raised to £80,000.

The 1897 season saw another significant step forward for the company. At the end of that year Captain Alec bought the old iron paddler *Glen Rosa*, and it would appear that he did so to exploit the trade which he and his brother had found on the Solent when they sent their three stars, *Westward Ho*, *Cambria* and *Britannia*, to the Diamond Jubilee Naval Review in June of the same year. The brothers ran excursions from Bournemouth and Southampton to view the fleet, and *Cambria* remained on the south coast for the latter part of the season. In 1898 *Cambria* and *Glen Rosa* were back again at Southampton, whence they ran excursions to Southsea, Bournemouth and the Isle of Wight, and in this same year the first cross-Channel excursions to France were introduced.

In 1899 there were even greater advances. John Gunn went out of business at Cardiff

and the Campbell fleet bought his *Bonnie Doon* and *Scotia*. Just previously they had bought another steel paddler, the *Slieve Donard*, which they renamed *Albion*, and these additions brought the total number of vessels up to ten—a formidable expansion in just 12 years' operations.

As the century turned, Campbell's continued their operations at Southampton, and for the first time met a commercial competitor who proved to be their equal. The Southampton, Isle of Wight & South of England Royal Mail Steam Packet Company possessed—and still does—the longest title of any steamship company in the business. In later years it was to be known as the Red Funnel Fleet but at the time when Campbell's operated in the Solent its vessels likewise carried a white funnel. For the purpose of this story we will refer to it as the Southampton Company.

In their fleet the Southampton Company had none other than *Lorna Doone*, which they had bought in 1898 from John Gunn. Later, in 1900, they added the new paddler *Balmoral*, which was to prove every bit as successful as Campbell's *Cambria*, and it was

6 (*above*) Westward Ho *and* Waverley *loading at Barry in the early years of this century*

7 (*below*) Lorna Doone, Bonnie Doon, Cambria, Westward Ho, Earl of Dunraven *and* Alexandra (*ex* Aquila) *at Ilfracombe in 1895. The superior quality of the two White Funnellers is very apparent in this picture*

probably a combination of the *Balmoral's* superiority, local loyalties to the Southampton Company and the Campbell brothers' growing interest in Brighton that led to the White Funnel ships leaving Southampton at the end of the 1902 season.

The long connection of P. & A. Campbell Ltd with the twin towns of Brighton and Hove began in 1901 and was to last for 56 years. *Cambria* had done a certain amount of charter work at the Sussex piers early in the 1901 season, and when the Brighton, Worthing & South Coast Steam Boat Company came on the market in the autumn of that year, Captains Peter and Alec bought it out, together with the two ships *Brighton Queen* and *Princess May*.

Brighton Queen was a splendid ship and, following modifications, served the company on the south coast until the outbreak of war in 1914. *Princess May* was much smaller and completely out of her class in the Campbell fleet, and it is not surprising that she was sold to some Italians in mid-1902. The company were obviously at this time rationalising their operations, because we find that in 1903 they sold both *Scotia* and *Lady Margaret*. The sale of the *Scotia* is understandable, since she was by this time an ancient vessel with out-of-date equipment, but it is hard to understand why the newer *Lady Margaret* was sold, to the Furness Railway Company. Probably Campbell's would have preferred to dispose of *Bonnie Doon*, but that ship's dubious reputation may have made it difficult to dispose of her.

We must now return to the Bristol Channel, where, after an interval of 6 years, serious competition was again forthcoming. This time the challenge came from a company that had solid financial backing and modern reliable ships. The Barry Railway Company began its steamship operations in 1905, following delays of several years while it forced an Act through Parliament to give it running rights in the Channel. Campbell's had been one of a number of objectors in both Houses of Parliament, and they pursued their objections even more vigorously when the Barry Company began its sailings.

The Barry Railway Steam Vessels Act, 1904, became law in the autumn of that year, and the company planned to operate three ships in the 1905 season under the popular title of the 'Red Funnel Line'. Initially the venture proved a success, but in August P. & A. Campbell Ltd initiated an action in the Chancery Division of the High Court seeking an injunction against the Barry Railway Company to stop it running steamships outside the limits of its Act.

Under the terms of its Act, the Barry Railway Company's ships were only permitted to sail between Barry and places on the south coast of the Channel between Weston and Ilfracombe inclusive. This applied during the whole year and there was a limited concession on excursions to other places in the summer season, always provided that the said excursions started and ended at Barry Pier. The Act cut out Cardiff and Bristol, two of the Channel's most lucrative runs, and the Barry Company tried to evade the restrictions in various ways. Their main ruse was to register their ships in the names of individuals who were either directors or shareholders of the Railway Company.

The full story of 'P. & A. Campbell Ltd and others v the Barry Railway Company and others' can be read in the law reports of the time, but the result was a lawsuit that went on for nearly two years, ended in 1907 with the Railway Company finally agreeing to operate the terms of the Act. It was a legal

8 *Railway challenger* Barry *fitting out at Clydebank in 1907*

victory for the White Funnel company that led to the inevitable commercial decline of its competitors.

The Barry company had two excellent ships in the *Gwalia* and the *Devonia* and both were to find their way eventually into Campbell ownership, but even this superior equipment did not prevent the enforced sale of its steamship interests in 1910 to a consortium of Cardiff coal owners, who in their turn sold *Devonia*, *Westonia* and *Barry* to Campbell's in December 1911. Despite the modernisation of the *Westonia* and her new name of *Tintern*, she was sold in 1912. With the purchase of the *Devonia* and the *Barry* and the delivery of the new *Lady Ismay* in 1911, *Tintern* was obviously surplus to requirements. However,

trade was such that Campbell's proceeded to build the *Glen Avon* in 1912 and the *Glen Usk* in 1914. These years saw the heyday of the company.

It is interesting to see the disposition of the ships for a typical season before World War I. On 31 May 1912 the *Western Daily Press* carried the following list:

Port	Ship	Captain
Bristol	Britannia	Taylor
	Westward Ho	Ashford
Cardiff	Lady Ismay	Chidzey
	Cambria	Livingstone
	Barry	Denman
	Devonia	Ryan
Newport	Albion	J. Webber
	Bonnie Doon	R. Webber
Barry	Waverley	Jerribob
Brighton	Brighton Queen	West
	Glen Rosa	James
Eastbourne	Ravenswood	MacFadyen

9 *Minesweeping gear fitted to* Devonia *in World War I*

Another alteration in the fleet before the outbreak of World War I was the sale of *Bonnie Doon* to Dutch breakers in August 1913.

The whole fleet was eventually taken into the Royal Navy during World War I and the individual records of service will be found in the section describing the ships. By 1917 every vessel was away on national duties and the Campbells chartered *Duchess of Devonshire* to keep the Cardiff-Weston ferry open.

When the war ended, three of the fleet had been lost by enemy action and three more were scrapped as unfit for reconditioning. Eight ships were left, therefore, when the company recommenced operations in the Bristol Channel in 1919. They did not return to Brighton until 1923.

In the 1919 season yet another competitor from Cardiff appeared in the shape of Messrs

W. H. Tucker, who were local tug owners. They brought two ships down from Lancashire, *Lady Moyra* and *Lady Evelyn*, the former being an old rival in that she was originally *Gwalia*, which we have met earlier in the story. Tucker's also brought in a screw steamer, *Robina*, under charter. By 1920, however, Campbell's had got their flyers back in operation in the shape of *Britannia*, *Cambria* and *Westward Ho*, and the Cardiff company eventually ceased operations in September 1921. The surviving two vessels went under the hammer in the middle of 1922 and were bought by the Campbell company. In the same season they also took delivery of *Glen Gower*, which was to be their only major purchase for the next 17 years. *Glen*

10 *Good business for* Glen Gower *and* Lady
Moyra *at Ilfracombe in 1926. Note that the
motor car has arrived!*

Gower went to Swansea, a station on which
the Campbells had intervened in 1920 with
Barry. It is surprising that they arrived at this
port at so late a date, particularly in view of
Alec Campbell's speech of 1891 referred to
earlier; but they never challenged Pockett's
and only came to Swansea when that company had ceased passenger operations.

The inter-war period was one of continued
commercial success, but changes were coming
in the company and 1928 was to see the death
of Captain Alec. Captain Peter outlived his
brother and died in 1938 when he was in his
eighties. (A biographical note of both founders

of the company will be found in the Appen-
dix.) There were variations in the vessels
used on the company's different services, but
generally the high standard of catering, com-
fort and reliability was maintained.

One interesting diversion was the operation
of *Westward Ho* from Torquay during the
1932 and 1933 seasons. It was the first venture of the company into the South Devon
coast on a permanent basis, and was to prove
abortive, although the company went to the
extent of buying up *Duke of Devonshire* to
stop her sailing in the area for a rival company.

It was not until the late 1930s that the
signs of trouble to come began to appear:
1939 saw *Devonia* laid up and already the
attractions of the motor car and motor coach

11 (above) Devonia and Brighton Belle at Boulogne between the wars. The latter appears to be using the international 'T' flag as a makeshift courtesy Tricolour!

12 (below) Bristol City Docks from the air in the 1930s. The ships are Glen Usk (bottom left) and Ravenswood. The Campbell fleet laid up here each winter until 1956, when the move to Cardiff was made

13 Devonia *in the heart of Bristol for the Coronation celebrations of King George VI in 1937*

excursions were making some inroads into the company's passenger figures. At this time the return fare to Ilfracombe was 8s or 10s 6d if you wished to go on to Lundy. The usual services were provided and there were cruises to special events. For example, *Glen Gower, Glen Usk, Brighton Queen* and *Devonia* were present at the Coronation Review in May 1937, and the entire fleet, with the exception of *Waverley* and *Westward Ho*, was in some way or other involved in the event, either running excursions or under charter to various organisations. A trip from Cardiff to Brighton on the *Brighton Queen*, returning by rail, cost 30s, while a rail ticket to Bournemouth, bus to Bournemouth Pier, a trip round the

fleet on the *Britannia*, and return to Bristol could all be got for 15s.

On 17 February 1939 readers of the Bristol papers were staggered to read that the company intended to build a screw steamer. The company announced that this giant would carry 2,000 passengers and was being built in Scotland specifically for their day trips to France from the south coast holiday resorts.

But Bristol was not to see the new acquisition until June 1947. On 3 September 1939 World War II broke out; the company had cancelled all its sailings on the previous day. In the holocaust that followed the entire fleet was pressed into service by the navy, only *Ravenswood* managing to operate a partial Cardiff-Weston ferry in early 1940; and when eventually the ships began to trickle back to Bristol in 1945 no less than five had been sunk and two more were scrapped because of their poor condition. The war record of the individual ships is given under Part 3: 'The Ships'.

Despite the war losses and the austerity period that followed the end of the conflict, the Board of the company boldly determined to rebuild the fleet of paddle steamers and announced orders for the two largest ships of that type ever constructed for the company. In the light of future events, it was a bold, even risky, decision, but the results were the Bristol-built *Bristol Queen* and *Cardiff Queen*, two fine ships which lasted until the late 1960s. *Ravenswood* reopened the services from Bristol on 11 April 1946 with an excursion to Walton Bay and Clevedon that was

14 Britannia *and* Bristol Queen *at Cardiff in 1955*

timed to leave at 3.30 pm. An hour before sailing time the queue of intending passengers stretched half a mile back along Hotwells Road, and despite the fact that some of the Channel piers, notably Weston, Clevedon and Ilfracombe, were not available, the early postwar years provided good support from the travelling public.

By 1947 *Cardiff Queen* had joined *Bristol Queen*, which had come out in the previous September. *Empress Queen*, the new screw ship, was also available, though she proved to be a white elephant throughout her career with the company. Denied her planned operations due to government currency restrictions on cross-Channel trips to France, she spent four seasons blundering alongside south coast piers for which she was not designed, and it came as no surprise when she was laid up at Bristol

and offered for sale. She eventually went to Greek buyers in March 1955.

The six paddle steamers soon settled down to services that were limited versions of the prewar runs. *Glen Gower* returned to Brighton in 1947, while the others operated in the Bristol Channel. Boiler trouble in *Britannia* during 1946 had led to a considerable reconstruction of that vessel, and when she returned in 1948, operating at Brighton, she possessed two funnels for the first time in her career. Traffic was reasonably plentiful in the late 1940s and early 1950s, despite the fact that many of the Channel piers were suffering from the results of wartime occupation by military authorities. Minehead Pier had completely disappeared. However, the piers reopened one by one and for a number of seasons operations were reasonably prosperous.

The first postwar signs of trouble appeared in 1951 when, for the first time since 1901, no Campbell steamer operated from Brighton, although three had been there the previous season. *Empress Queen* was transferred to Torquay and put on the Channel Islands excursions run, but the venture was not successful, as the ship proved almost impossible to fill, even in the height of the season.

In the following year Campbell's were back on the south coast with *Cardiff Queen* at Brighton and she was joined for the Coronation Review at Spithead by *Bristol Queen* and *Glen Gower*. This was the last occasion on which three Campbell steamers were to be on the south coast at the same time, and although 1954 saw the resumption of day trips to France, the company made a loss on the whole

season of nearly £54,000.

The 1955 season had much better weather, and 40,000 more passengers were carried, including the highest figure to Ilfracombe since 1924. But, as the chairman, Roy Boucher, pointed out, costs were five times their 1924 values while fares had only doubled. Nevertheless a profit of £26,656 was made.

The season of 1956 marks a turning point in the story of the White Funnel Fleet. The weather was bad and a meeting of shareholders at Bristol on 26 July was informed that the loss was likely to be around £74,000 for the season, bringing the company's liabilities to nearly a quarter of a million. Drastic action was taken by the Board to reduce this deficit. The company's headquarters were moved from Bristol to Cardiff, which city now provided the bulk of travelling passengers, and the lease of the Underfall Yard from the Port of Bristol Authority was discontinued. Thus ended the connection of the company with the City and County of Bristol, which had started in the 1880s, and many Bristolians felt that part of their town had been lost as a result. As if to rub salt into the wound, Bristol's own *Britannia* went to the breakers in December 1956, and although the Port of Bristol Authority tried to assist the company by giving it very preferential rates for the use of Hotwells landing stage, sailings from Bristol were to be sparse in the years that followed.

In 1957 the company withdrew from Newport, and this also was to be its final year at Brighton, where *Crested Eagle* was chartered from General Steam Navigation. *Glen Gower*, *Glen Usk* and *Bristol Queen* were all laid up for seasons in the late 1950s, and a receiver, W. Walker, was appointed in 1959. However, the entire assets and liabilities were taken over by George Nott Industries Limited, among whose other interests are the Townsend-

15 *The classic beauty of Brunel's Clifton Suspension Bridge frames* Ravenswood *as she leaves Bristol towards the end of her career*

16 Valete. *A grey day as* Britannia *makes her last sailing from Bristol*

Thoresen Ferry Group. The deal with George Nott Industries was announced on 8 December 1959 and confirmed by the shareholders on the last day of the decade. The Coventry-based company immediately announced that excursion activities would continue and one of the directors, R. B. Wickenden, told the press that there was 'still a demand in the Bristol Channel for these services on a somewhat less lavish scale'.

With this industrial giant now backing the company, the early 1960s saw a new lease of life. As a sign of things to come a motor vessel first appeared in the Bristol Channel services in 1963, and there was an experiment with hovercraft in the same year, when a service was operated from Weston to Penarth. This was a pioneering venture in company with Westland Aircraft Limited and was not repeated, although P. & A. Campbell have operated these unlovely vehicles on the south coast in recent years. The motor vessel already referred to was *St Trillo*, which had been

bought, together with the goodwill of the Llandudno excursion trade, when the Liverpool & North Wales Steamship Company went out of business at the end of the 1962 season. Operations in North Wales started in the summer of 1963 in cooperation with the Isle of Man S.P.Co Ltd.

A further addition was another motor vessel, *Vecta*, which was bought from the Southampton Company at the end of 1965. Renamed *Westward Ho*, she carried out most of the company's services in the Bristol Channel in the late 1960s. Both motor ships were registered under the ownership of Townsend Ferries, a Nott subsidiary.

The arrival of the motor vessels and the reduced passenger traffic sealed the fate of the paddle steamers. Beautiful as these ships were, their high fuel consumption and manning requirements made them thoroughly uneconomic. *Cardiff Queen* went in 1966 and *Bristol Queen* a year later, following a spate of technical trouble. Thus the 1968 season saw the company with motor vessels only for the first time in its career, and further strength was gained by chartering the Cornish vessel

Queen of the Isles for some of the long-distance work at North Wales and the Isles of Scilly run.

The activities of *Queen of the Isles* demonstrate the opportunist policy of the company in these latter years, in that the ships sometimes operated 'one off' excursions each year to cater for the enthusiasts for coastal travel who still remained. An inaugural exursion to Penzance and the Scilly Isles was made in 1963 and has operated annually ever since, and *Queen of the Isles* made trips to places as far afield as Hastings on the south coast.

This latter vessel also operated from Hastings and Eastbourne in the summer of 1969. Day trips to the Isle of White were a feature of the programme, and a number of excursions from London's Tower Pier to Margate and Southend were operated. It proved to be the first and last White Funnel season on the Thames, as the services were not repeated in 1970.

However, these activities did not prevent the further withdrawal of the traditional excursions. *St Trillo* was laid up at the end of the 1969 season, and this was also the company's last full season in North Wales. *Queen of the Isles* was sold overseas by her owners in 1970, and 1971 saw the final sailings of the second *Westward Ho*. This ship had carried out valiant work since her purchase by the company in 1965, but she was now over 30 years old and her engines in particular were showing their age.

In a further rationalisation to cater for the reduced public demand the company announced in September 1971 that they were withdrawing almost entirely from the Upper Bristol Channel. This decision was taken not only because of the sparse trade in that area, but also because the condition of the piers at Cardiff and Barry were such that only very

costly repairs would make them safe for future public use. Additionally, the century-old pier at Clevedon had collapsed during test in the autumn of 1970. The company, therefore, announced that, apart from occasional calls at Weston-super-Mare and Bristol, it would in future operate from Swansea and the West Welsh piers to Lundy and Ilfracombe. Occasional charter work would still be carried out, such as the traditional tender to Swedish-America Cruise Liners at Bristol, Llandudno and the Isle of Man, and the usual excursion to the Isles of Scilly was announced for October 1972. The traditional link with the south coast would be maintained by the continued use of the company's booking agent facilities for day trips to France on the Townsend and Thoresen ferries. The actual services are now operated by the motor ship *Balmoral* —an ironic touch as this ship is named after the paddle steamer that first clashed with *Cambria* in the Solent over 70 years ago.

Nevertheless, the company can take pride in its history and its record of service to thousands of excursionists, past and present. The blue and white burgee and the shiny white funnels have appeared consistently in western coastal waters of the British Isles for well over three-quarters of a century. No other private company can offer such a record, and even today, long after the paddle wheels of the *Britannia* and the *Cambria*, the *Westward Ho* and the *Devonia* have ceased to stir the muddy waters of the Avon, Bristol people recall those spring mornings when they took a tram along St Georges Road to Hotwells, where the immaculate *Britannia* would be waiting to cast off for another trip 'down 'Combe with Campbells'. Soon the telegraphs would ring and another White Funnel excursion was under way. Memories of those golden days and lovely ships will die hard.

2 THE RIVAL FLEETS

As already recorded, there were a number of operators of pleasure excursions in business in the Bristol Channel when Campbell's *Waverley* arrived in 1887. They ranged in scope from the 'outing' organiser who chartered the best vessel he could afford, to large commercial concerns like the Great Western Railway, which operated the ferry *Chepstow* in occasional trips from Bristol to Ilfracombe. Between these extremes there were a number of private owners based on the larger Channel ports and several companies with 'fleets', all of whom operated genuine pleasure steamers from the mid-1880s until Campbell's last competitor ceased operations in 1921.

Apart from the larger vessels, a large number of tugs also intervened in the trade, and at least two, King's *Merrimac* and the Cardiff-owned *Earl of Dunraven*, lasted until 1895. The former ran excursions from Bristol to Chepstow at 1s 6d return, while the *Earl* was a regular caller at Ilfracombe from Cardiff. The activities of these owners and companies are best related to the ports on which they were based.

Swansea

The principal operators from this port were the Pockett family—shipowners, masters and agents through several generations. They engaged in the general cargo and passenger trade of the Channel and specialised in the Ilfracombe and Bristol runs from Swansea. It was not until after the death of Captain William Pockett in 1890 that the company engaged in excursion work wholly for its own sake. The company re-formed under Bristol ownership as Pockett's Bristol Channel S.P. Co, and the ships *Velindra*, *Brighton* and *Mavis* all operated in the trade. *Brighton* lasted until requisitioned by the Admiralty in 1914, but Pockett's did not operate passenger ships after World War I.

From 1892 to 1896 a James Jones operated from Swansea with two vessels that he successively named *Alexandra*, and there was an intervention of a few weeks by the Clyde-owned *Victoria* in 1891. After Mr Jones there was a pause and Pockett's had no rivals until 1905, when a Mr Richards introduced the old railway steamer *Normandy*, which he operated until 1909. There was a final spurt of activity in 1920 when W. K. David used the old Clyde steamer *Lady Rowena*, but she lasted only the season and did not put in many sailings at that. In the same year P. & A. Campbell commenced sailings from Swansea. One is left to speculate why they left Pockett's unchallenged for so many years and only arrived in Swansea when the local firm had left the passenger trade.

17 Pockett's veteran Velindra *at Ilfracombe in 1889*

Barry

This port will always be associated with the Barry Railway Company and its various subsidiaries in their battle to commercial death with Campbell's during the Edwardian decade. The story has been related elsewhere in this book (pp21-2).

Cardiff

At the turn of the nineteenth century Cardiff was a major international port, engaged in handling a major international necessity—coal. Despite the grim conditions imposed on those who mined it, its very existence ensured great prosperity in the area, and there seems to have been no lack of people with sufficient money to invest in the hazardous business of running excursion steamers. Few of these small owners lasted long, however, but the partners Frederick Edwards and George Robertson emerged as major competitors of the Campbell brothers in the late 1880s and early 1890s. Edwards started as early as 1883 with *Lady Margaret* (she was to have two successors with the same

name), and Edwards & Robertson's *Lorna Doone* of 1891 was to become one of the most famous paddle steamers ever constructed.

That ship apart, their equipment never quite matched that of the Bristol firm and in 1895 they sold out to another Cardiff owner, James Gunn. He operated until 1899, from which year Campbell's remained supreme at Cardiff until the Barry Railway's challenge in 1905.

A serious attempt to drive the White Funnel vessels off the Cardiff station was made by the tug owners W. H. Tucker & Co after World War I. Operating as the Yellow Funnel Co, they offered services with two useful paddlers, *Lady Evelyn* and *Lady Moyra*, and they also chartered the screw vessel *Robina*. The venture was not successful, however, particularly as more White Funnel vessels returned from war service, and Tucker's ceased trading as excursion ship owners in the autumn of 1921.

Campbell's were left with exactly 50 years more at Cardiff, withdrawing from the station in September 1971.

Bristol

We have already seen how George Nurse's charter of *Bonnie Doon* in 1886 led directly to the arrival of *Waverley* in 1887 and the direct intervention of the Campbell family in the Bristol trade. From 1890 onwards Campbell's reigned supreme at Bristol, but one or two brave spirits brought their vessels up the Avon to challenge the all-conquering White Funnellers.

In 1894 a local syndicate chartered the Bournemouth paddler *Brodick Castle*, but her all-black hull and upperworks must have seemed distinctly dowdy to Bristolians, who did not patronise her in any numbers, and she was soon back on the South Coast.

From 1901 to 1903, an excursion organiser, Edwin Hunt, used an old Clyde steamer, *Heather Belle*, at Bristol under his own flag, and in 1905 chartered the diminutive *Ribble Queen*. Hunt's ventures appear to have been unprofitable, however, and he was the last of the private owners to base himself at Bristol with sea-going pleasure vessels.

18 Brighton *moored at St George's Road, Bristol*

3 THE SHIPS

THE FLEET OF P. & A. CAMPBELL LTD

The vessels are listed in the order in which they entered the fleet.

WAVERLEY (I)

Type	Steel Paddle Steamer
GRT	258 tons
Length	205.0ft
Breadth	21.2ft
Depth	7.5ft
Builders	H. McIntyre & Co Ltd, Paisley
Engine Makers	Hutson & Corbett
Engine Type	D1 cyl, 52-60in
NHP	99
Yard No	123
Speed	19 knots

Following the turn in the family fortunes in 1884, Captain Robert Campbell ordered *Waverley* for the Glasgow-Kilmun trade and she came into service in 1885. However, the ship proved too big to fill on this commuter route—a problem that has dogged Holy Loch operators to this day—and so Captain Campbell put her in the excursion trade from Ayr.

As already mentioned, *Waverley's* speed led to her being chartered in 1887, and she came south to the Bristol Channel under the command of Captain Alec Campbell. Following the decision to move permanently to Bristol in the spring of 1888, *Waverley* was the main weapon of the Campbell armoury in the fight for the Channel trade until the advent of *Ravenswood* in 1891.

A good looking ship, with a single acting diagonal engine and a haystack boiler, *Waverley* spent most of her career in the Bristol

19 Waverley (I) *in her final form. Contrast her appearance in Plates 1 and 3*

Channel, being demoted to the shorter runs as larger and more powerful steamers were built. She was reboilered in 1901. As first constructed, she had square saloon windows in typical Clyde fashion, but these were replaced with circular ports in 1911. *Waverley* spent the 1911 season on the south coast operating from Brighton, Eastbourne, and Hastings, but was back in the Bristol Channel for the 1912 season.

She kept her civilian status during the early years of World War I and was used to keep the Weston-Cardiff ferry open until the end of the 1916 season. The ship was requisitioned on 30 May 1917 and fitted out at Swansea, whence she operated as a minesweeper until sent to the Thames Estuary. For her war service she was renamed *Way* to avoid confusion with the North British Railway's paddle steamer *Waverley*, already serving in the Navy. On release by the Admiralty on 17 May 1919 she was surveyed, and as the survey showed she was not worth repairing, was sold for breaking up after a useful life of 34 years.

	RAVENSWOOD
Type	Steel Paddle Steamer
GRT	391 tons
Length	215.0ft
Breadth	24.1ft
Depth	8.5ft
Builders	S. McKnight & Co Ltd, Ayr
Engine Makers	1. Hutson & Son
	2. Barclay, Curle & Co Ltd
Engine Type	1. D1 cyl, 56-72in
	2. CD 2 cyls, $25\frac{1}{2}$in, 50-54in
NHP	205
	153
Yard No	28
Speed	16.5 knots

After *Waverley's* success in opening Campbell's Bristol Channel services, it was obvious that a new steamer was required to exploit the rapidly growing trade. *Ravenswood* was ordered in 1890 and launched on 27 April 1891. She arrived in Bristol in early July and made her first voyage, to Chepstow, on 3 July. *Ravenswood* was the first steamer specifically designed for service in the Bristol Channel, but she retained a typical Clyde rig and came out with a Scots name. Perhaps it was still too early for the Campbell brothers to admit that they were finally committed to the Bristol Channel, although they registered this new ship there.

Much rebuilt over the years, *Ravenswood* was a very successful steamer that ran in all for sixty-four seasons, if one includes the war years. The main contract for her construction went to Hutson & Son of Glasgow, who subcontracted the hull to Messrs McKnight at Ayr, an arrangement repeated in the three following steamers. When *Ravenswood* came out, she had a single-cylinder engine whose 56in diameter bore made it the largest ever of its type. This machine was supplied by two haystack boilers which gave the ship twin funnels forward of the bridge. She had an open foredeck, which she retained for her entire career, but she received new engines and boilers in 1909, reducing the funnels to one. Later her square saloon windows were refitted with round ports. The Clyde practice of large square saloon windows proved impractical in ships that often had to round Land's End in spring gales while on route to the south coast resorts, and after World War I the Campbell fleet retained small round ports, apart from the three steamers that came from the Barry Railway Company.

Ravenswood's initial services were mainly on the Bristol-Ilfracombe run but she served on all the company's routes at one time or another. She was in collision with *Lorna Doone* on 5 June 1893 (see p16). The ship sailed on the south coast from 1912 to 1914, being based at Brighton and Hastings, and again in 1923, when she made a number of crossings to Boulogne. For this service she received a wireless installation and a stump mast. In 1926, however, *Ravenswood* returned to the Bristol Channel where she remained for the rest of her civilian career.

Her war service opened on 1 July 1915, when she was requisitioned as a minesweeper, and she returned to Bristol in March 1919, having served throughout the war at Dover. When World War II broke out in 1939, *Ravenswood* was not called up immediately and, after a sporadic attempt to keep the Weston-Cardiff ferry open—an effort swiftly ended by the Luftwaffe—she was laid up until 1941 at Bristol where she was damaged in an air raid. She then became an auxiliary anti-aircraft ship stationed at Belfast. From there she went to Plymouth as a special service vessel, returning to Bristol in April 1945. A long refit by Messrs Charles Hill at Albion

20 (*above*) Ravenswood *in her original rig entering Bristol with a full load*

21 (*below*) *Aground on Lavernock Point. Ravenswood by 1909 had one funnel and her bridge had been moved forward. After her saloon windows were replaced with round ports, she was little altered until 1946*

22 (*above*) Ravenswood *between the wars*

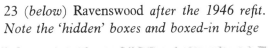

23 (*below*) Ravenswood *after the 1946 refit.*
Note the 'hidden' boxes and boxed-in bridge

Dockyard followed, and she received new paddle boxes, which were nothing like as decorative as their predecessors, and a 'boxed-in' bridge. She reopened Campbell services from Bristol on 11 April 1946 with a short cruise to Walton Bay, Clevedon. The sailing was timed for 3.30 pm departure, and an hour before this time a queue formed at Hotwells landing stage and stretched for half a mile along the Portway.

Ravenswood spent the rest of her career in the Bristol Channel services until, in May 1955, she failed to pass a Board of Trade survey and was not considered worthy of economic refit. She left Bristol finally on 20 October 1955 for breaking up at Newport.

SEA BREEZE	
Type	Iron Paddle Steamer
GRT	206 tons
Length	207.7ft
Breadth	19.2ft
Depth	7.4ft
Builders	Caird & Co Ltd, Greenock
Engine Makers	Blackwood & Gordon
Engine Type	D1 cyl, 49-54in
NHP	136
Yard No	210
Speed	12 knots

24 Sea Breeze *at Brighton. Photographs of this vessel in English waters are rare. None are known to exist of her in Campbell colours*

By 1893 the Campbell brothers were so well established at Bristol that they were able to turn to new routes for expansion. The Cardiff-Weston ferry was a long-established Bristol Channel excursion route and Campbell's first entered that trade by chartering the iron paddler *Sea Breeze*. She ran in Captain Alec's name from mid-June until the end of September and was a warning of things to come to the established Welsh companies on the route.

Sea Breeze was launched 12 August 1877 and began her career as *Adela*, belonging to Captain Alexander Campbell of Rothesay. She served in his Wemyss Bay operations until 1891 when she was bought by the Brighton, Worthing & South Coast Steam Boat Company, which operated her for two years and renamed her *Sea Breeze*. She possessed a single diagonal engine which reputedly had been retrieved from an earlier steamer called the *Lady Gertrude*. This simple piece of machinery had an unfortunate knack of jamming in the top-dead-centre position when she was at slow speed and it usually chose to do so as *Sea Breeze* was approaching a pier. The ship was nearly wrecked on one occasion on the Clyde, and the engine jammed again off Brighton pier, fortunately without serious results. Captain Alec Campbell did not charter *Sea Breeze* again after 1893. It seems she was then laid up until sold to French operators, Le Banque Transatlantique, at Marseilles in 1896 and renamed *La Corse*. Her ultimate fate is obscure, but she does not appear in the registers after 1903.

WESTWARD HO (I)

Type	Steel Paddle Steamer
GRT	438 tons
Length	225.0ft
Breadth	26.1ft
Depth	9.5ft
Builders	S. McKnight & Co Ltd, Ayr
Engine Makers	Hutson & Son
Engine Type	CD 2 cyls, 36in, 64-66in
NHP	277
Yard No	42
Speed	20.5 knots

Three years after the introduction of *Ravenswood* the Campbell brothers returned to the same two contractors for their next ship. They gave her an uncompromisingly West Country name *Westward Ho*, and she was the first 'modern' vessel of the fleet in every sense of the word: the promenade deck was carried right up to the bow, the bridge was placed forward of the funnel and twin-cylinder compound diagonal engines were fitted to a design that was to become standard throughout the fleet. After *Westward Ho* no major technical developments in the design of the company's paddle steamers occurred until the arrival of *Bristol Queen* in 1946.

Westward Ho was launched on 7 April 1894 and went into service that summer. She replaced *Ravenswood* on the Bristol-Ilfracombe run on Saturday, 16 June, and as early as 27 July made her first run to Penzance. Always an attractive and popular steamer, she came out with square saloon windows forward. In 1897 she attended the Spithead naval review celebrating Queen Victoria's Diamond Jubilee but, surprisingly, no further review visits were made in the course of her 51-year career. On 19 August 1907, while alongside Clevedon pier at midnight, *Westward Ho* blew a steam pipe and a potentially dangerous situation was only avoided by the prompt action of the Chief Engineer, though a crew member was badly burnt. Passengers were taken off by *Ravenswood*, and when *Westward Ho* finally arrived at Bristol,

25 (above) Westward Ho (I) off Avonmouth in 1912. The naval funnel cowl is the only alteration from her original rig. Note the white deck-edge strake by which she can always be distinguished

26 (below) Westward Ho (I) passing Pill, the pilot village on the Avon, sometime in the 1930s

a crowd turned out to applaud the crew and sing the Doxology on the quayside. The ship was reboiled in 1912 when a naval pattern cruiser funnel cowl was fitted.

Westward Ho served in the Royal Navy from 2 December 1914 to 1 April 1919. She was equipped as a minesweeper, and had a mainmast fitted, but this was removed in 1920. The ship saw action in the North Sea on 15 August 1915 when, as a member of the minesweeping flotillas based on Grimsby, she and some of her colleagues were in action with a U-boat. Later in the war she was transferred to the Tyne and renamed *Westward Queen*, and, later still, *Westhope*.

When refitted for civilian use in 1920, her saloon windows were removed and the standard round ports used in all the Campbell fleet were fitted, *Westward Ho* being one of the last ships to be so converted. *Cambria's* wireless installation was removed and refitted in *Westward Ho* in 1932 when the latter vessel opened new Campbell services from Plymouth and Torquay. These services were repeated in 1933 but, proving to be unprofitable, were abandoned after that season. *Westward Ho* also operated at Brighton in 1931 and also as a relief steamer for the *Brighton Belle* when that ship broke down at the end of the 1934 season.

The second period of war service occurred between 13 September 1939 and 15 March 1946. *Westward Ho* served under her own name for the whole period and was at one time flagship of the 7th Minesweeping Flotilla, based on the Tyne and later on the Forth. She took part in the Dunkirk evacuation, being officially credited with the rescue of 1,686 troops and suffering slight bomb damage in the process. Later in the war she was laid up in the Dart and used as an accommodation ship. A number of ugly sheds

appeared on her promenade deck and she deteriorated so much that she had to be towed to Bristol when released by the Admiralty. Her condition was then found to be so bad that it was not economic to refit her, and she was towed from Bristol on 31 July 1946 to be broken up by Messrs Cashmore at Newport, Mon.

CAMBRIA

Type	Steel Paddle Steamer
GRT	420 tons
Length	225.0ft
Breadth	26.1ft
Depth	9.4ft
Builders	H. McIntyre & Co Ltd, Alloa
Engine Makers	Hutson & Son
Engine Type	CD 2 cyls, 37in, 67-66in
NHP	304
Yard No	144
Speed	20.5 knots

Cambria came out for the 1895 season as a slightly enlarged version of *Westward Ho*. If the Welsh excursion companies had any remaining doubts that the Campbell brothers were moving in on their trade, the name of this steamer quickly dispelled them. Rather incongruously, she carried the arms of the City of Ayr on her paddle boxes, even though she was built at Alloa on the Forth on the west side of Scotland. For years after her launch on 10 April 1895 a story persisted in the Bristol area that the Campbell brothers literally 'hijacked' the ship from McIntyre's yard at Alloa when that company was about to go into liquidation, having no intention of allowing their fine new steamer to be sold to pay creditors of the ailing shipyard. They took a crew north to the yard, sailed overnight and brought *Cambria* round to the Clyde for final fitting out.

27 (*above*) Cambria *as built*

28 (*left*) *After gale damage to her saloon windows,* Cambria *was replated and appeared with round ports*

29 (*below left*) *In this picture* Cambria *has acquired a funnel cowl and post-*Titanic *lifeboats*

Cambria served on the Cardiff-Ilfracombe route for most of her first season, though she did make occasional trips to Bristol, and it was during one of these, on 30 May 1896, that she was involved in a fatal accident—one of the very few that have occurred in Bristol Channel paddle-steamer history. Under the command of the celebrated Captain John West she had left Hotwells landing stage and was proceeding down the Avon, towing two boatmen who had 'hitched' a lift by tying their boat to *Cambria*'s stern for a tow down river, a common practice in those days. Unfortun-

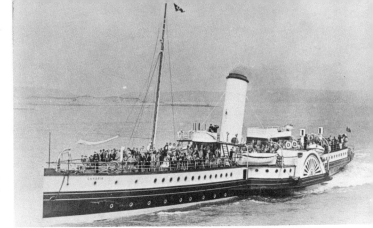

ately, at the Horseshoe Bend, Captain West was forced to go astern because of a ship coming up river, and *Cambria* ran the boat down. One of the boatmen, John Calloway, was drowned.

Cambria soon proved that she was a fast ship, but local enthusiasts still argue whether she or *Britannia* was the fastest ship Campbell's ever owned. Certainly Captain Alec was not satisfied with her speed at first, and in 1898 new floats were fitted to her paddle wheels. After that she was always listed among the fastest merchant ships in the world in the early years of this century.

Several structural alterations took place during *Cambria's* career. In August 1908 she

30 (*above right*) Cambria *after her final refit*

31 (*right*) Cambria's *paddle box, 29 June 1939*

31a (*below*) Cambria *as HMS* Plinlimmon *in 1942*

received a severe battering in a gale off Hartland Point and, on the same voyage, was damaged by flotsam near Portland Bill. The large saloon windows were broken in, and early opportunity was taken to replace them with round ports. A new boiler was fitted in 1912, and she was reboiled again in the summer of 1935, the latter refit putting her out of action for the 1935 season. She emerged in 1936 with a much larger funnel. She had received the company's standard cruiser cowl in 1914, and a stump mainmast in 1921 when radio was fitted, but that mast was removed in 1932.

In the summer of 1897 *Cambria* was at Spithead for the Naval Review of 28 June, and was sent back to the south coast in August of the same year, to be stationed at Southampton, where she remained until the end of the 1902 season. During this period she ran excursions to Bournemouth and Cherbourg, and one in 1902 to Boulogne. At Southampton her 'races' with the Southampton company's *Balmoral* became famous, and crowds would gather at Bournemouth to see which of the two fliers would arrive back first from Cherbourg. When Campbell's eventually withdrew from Southampton at the end of the 1902 season, *Cambria* went back to the Bristol Channel and remained there for the rest of her career, except for war service and one season at Brighton in 1908.

In World War I *Cambria* served from September 1914 until May 1919 under the name of *Cambridge* to avoid confusion with the railway steamer *Cambria*. She fitted out at Devonport and served as a minesweeper on the east coast, first at Grimsby and then on the Tyne, being involved in the action with UB4 on 15 August 1915 (along with *Westward Ho*, p43).

Confined to the Bristol Channel in the inter-war period, *Cambria* made headlines on 12 July 1926 when she ran aground in fog at Rilledge Point near Ilfracombe; 400 passengers were taken off by local boatmen and the Ilfracombe Lifeboat, and no one, including *Cambria*, was the worse for the incident. The ship floated off at high tide.

With the outbreak of war in 1939 *Cambria* was again converted to a minesweeper, this time at Messrs Charles Hill's Albion Dockyard in Bristol. She was in the Dunkirk operations and served on the Tyne until 1942, when she was converted to an anti-aircraft vessel. She was paid off in June 1943 at Harwich and later laid up in the Thames, where she suffered a bad fire in August 1946. By this time her condition was such that she did not return to Bristol but was broken up by Messrs Ward at Grays in Essex.

32 Lady Margaret *in the Avon*

LADY MARGARET

Type	Steel Paddle Steamer
GRT	369 tons
Length	210.0ft
Breadth	25.0ft
Depth	8.7ft
Builders	A. MacMillan & Son Ltd, Dumbarton
Engine Makers	D. Rowan & Son
Engine Type	CD 2 cyls, 28in, 64-54in
NHP	251
Yard No	335
Speed	17 knots

Lady Margaret was launched on 12 June 1895, but sources disagree about which company she ran for during that season. Certainly she was ordered and built for the Lady Margaret Steam Ship Company, a subsidiary of the Penarth Pier Company. Some records show that her owners operated her on their own account in opposition to both Campbell's and Edwards & Robertson, but others say that she was managed by the latter company and appeared in its colours. She was a fine looking ship and came up to the high standard that Campbell's in particular were setting in the Bristol Channel. However, when Edwards & Robertson went out of business at the end of the 1895 season, her owners decided not to run her the following year and sold her in March 1896 to the Bristol company.

Lady Margaret was used by Campbell's in the Bristol Channel only; she operated from Bristol and on the Cardiff-Weston ferry. In 1903 she was sold to the Furness Railway Company for use on their ferry services between the Lancashire ports of Barrow and Fleetwood, though the sale of this relatively new steamer in preference to the older *Bonnie Doon* is difficult to explain. The Campbell fleet certainly had surplus tonnage at this

stage of its history, and it may be that no one wanted to buy *Bonnie Doon* anyway, in view of that vessel's reputation. It has also been alleged that Campbell's found *Lady Margaret* too slow and too heavy on fuel.

The Furness Railway Company ran *Lady Margaret* for only 5 years. In 1908 they sold her to the Admiralty for tender duties and she remained in Government ownership until sold for breaking up in 1923.

BRITANNIA

Type	Steel Paddle Steamer
GRT	459 tons
Length	230.0ft
Breadth	26.6ft
Depth	9.6ft
Builders	S. McKnight & Co Ltd, Ayr
Engine Makers	Hutson & Son
Engine Type	CD 2 cyls, 37in, 67-66in
NHP	304
Yard No	48
Speed	21 knots

33 Britannia *as originally designed*

The most famous of all the Campbell steamers was launched on 14 May 1896 and named *Britannia*, an appropriate title for the vessel that was the company's flagship until after World War II. Registered at Bristol, she made her maiden voyage from Hotwells on 27 June 1896 and, outclassing every other steamer, she was adopted by thousands of Bristolians as 'our *Britannia*'. She carried the head of Britannia on her paddle boxes. For almost her entire career she operated the company's 'blue riband' Bristol-Ilfracombe service.

Britannia underwent a number of major structural changes during a career of 60 years. Apart from wartime modifications, she was largely unchanged until 1921, when new boilers were fitted, the large square saloon windows were changed to round ports and a stump mainmast was erected to carry the new wireless installation. She continued thus until 1935, when she was once again re-boilered, emerging with a much larger funnel. Two new lifeboats and a deckhouse were provided at the same time, and many people thought that this refit greatly enhanced her appearance.

34 Britannia *as rebuilt in 1935. The slab-sided funnel is prominent*

After World War II *Britannia* experienced more boiler trouble, and in 1948 she was greatly changed. The two additional lifeboats and the deckhouse added in 1935 were removed, but, more important, she now sported two funnels to cope with a double-ended Fairfield boiler. She was also converted to oil fuel. Even with this complete facelift she still looked a splendid steamer, and was reputedly a knot faster—remarkable when one remembers she was good for 20 knots throughout her career. Just before the end of a long life, in 1954 she was given a full mainmast to meet the new regulations concerning riding lights.

There have been many arguments about *Britannia's* speed, but there is little doubt she was the fastest paddler in the fleet. On her trials she is reported to have achieved a mean $19\frac{3}{4}$ knots for four runs over the measured mile, with seats, gear and stores on board, though ships are usually 'tried' light. She made the Penarth to Weston run in 23 minutes with ropes landed (*Cambria's* best was 24 minutes with no ropes ashore), and Cardiff-Weston and return in 1 hour 3 minutes. Other examples of her performance are as follows:

Cardiff-Ilfracombe (43 miles) 2 hours 3 minutes with ropes ashore on neap tide at dead ebb.

Ilfracombe-Weston ($43\frac{1}{2}$ miles) 1 hour 56 minutes with tide. Left 3 lengths astern of *Devonia*—arrived 6 minutes ahead.

Although *Britannia* was traditionally a Bristol-based ship, she did make excursions occasionally to Penzance and the Scillies, and always went south to Bournemouth for the naval reviews at Spithead. She was there in

35 (*above*) *Pictured at Bristol on her return from World War II*, Britannia *as the AA vessel HMS* Skiddaw

36 (*below*) *Sporting two masts and two funnels*, Britannia *on 1 July 1954*

1897, twice in 1902 and was back again in 1935, 1937 and 1952.

Britannia was called up like the rest of the fleet in 1914 and left Bristol on 5 February 1915 for service on the Clyde and later on the east coast of Scotland. Farr says that she was renamed HMS *Briton* for part of this service, and this is likely, as the Navy already possessed a battleship called *Britannia*. He also claims that she was present at the surrender of the German Fleet to Beatty in November 1918, but the company's records do not support this.

After the war *Britannia* refitted on the Clyde and returned to her normal duties. She was trapped in the Floating Harbour with a number of other ships when the steamer *Ettrick* went aground in fog in the Avon in June 1926 and capsized, blocking the river.

On 13 September 1939 *Britannia* again entered the Royal Navy, this time as HMS *Skiddaw*. Fitted out at Albion Dockyard, Bristol, she joined the 7th Minesweeping Flotilla and served on the Tyne. She missed the Dunkirk evacuation but, following conversion to an anti-aircraft ship in 1942, she was in the Normandy invasion fleet in 1944 and finally returned to Bristol on 7 May 1945.

Britannia made her first postwar sailing on 1 June 1946 but serious boiler trouble developed in July of that year and she missed the 1947 season while Hills rebuilt her. She spent 1948 and 1949 at Brighton, but the failing south coast trade led to her recall to the Bristol Channel for 1950, where she spent much of her time at Swansea until her final trip on 26 September 1956. The company then announced she was to be laid up. No one in the Bristol area imagined that their old favourite had made her last commercial voyage, but the end came on 7 December 1956, when she was towed to Newport for breaking up.

GLEN ROSA

Type	Iron Paddle Steamer
GRT	223 tons
Length	206.1ft
Breadth	20.0ft
Depth	7.5ft
Builders	Caird & Co Ltd
Engine Makers	Builders
Engine Type	D1 cyl, 50-72in
NHP	120
Yard No	208
Speed	16 knots

Glen Rosa was a typical Clyde paddle steamer of the 1870s, built for the Arran services of Messrs Shearer Brothers & Ritchie. Any ship that failed to make money never stayed long on the Clyde, and *Glen Rosa* came south in 1881 when she was sold to the Thames & Channel Steam Ship Company. The ship then changed hands four times. First she was bought by the London Steam Boat Company (later the River Thames Steam Boat Company) in 1883, and in 1888 she is recorded as passing into the ownership of the Victoria Steam Boat Association. They gave her a telescopic funnel, presumably for passing under Thames bridges, and also operated her under charter at Brighton in 1895. Captain Alec Campbell bought her on his own account in 1897 but transferred her to the family firm in 1898.

Glen Rosa's first season in Campbell ownership was spent at Southampton in 1898. She came south again to Brighton in 1903 and served there every season until 1912. Her very large paddle wheels, which extended below the keel, were modified so that she could operate at half tide in the Bristol Channel, particularly on the Weston-Cardiff ferry. In April 1911 she received round ports, a new saloon aft and a new funnel.

37 Glen Rosa *in the Avon*

Following the outbreak of World War I, *Glen Rosa* kept the skeleton services in the Bristol Channel going in company with *Waverley*, but she was called up for mine-sweeping duties on 30 May 1917. Stationed at Swansea, she remained in Government employ until 23 March 1919, when it was judged uneconomic to refit her for civilian use and she was sold for scrap at Bristol to Messrs Joseph Pugsley.

	SCOTIA
Type	Iron Paddle Steamer
GRT	260 tons
Length	211.2ft
Breadth	21.8ft
Depth	8.3ft
Builders	H. McIntyre & Co Ltd, Paisley
Engine Makers	W. King & Co
Engine Type	S St 2 cyls, 45-48in
NHP	135
Yard No	48
Speed	14 knots

This remarkable looking steamer had four previous owners before Campbell's bought her in 1899, when the Cardiff shipowner John Gunn went out of business. She was built originally for Captain William Buchanan, and in her early years did not possess the forecastle that later ruined her appearance. *Scotia* is remembered as the last ship to be built with the 'double steeple' type of engine, a design very popular in Clyde steamers of the middle of the last century. Captain Buchanan used

38 John York's striking shot of Scotia *in mid-Channel*

the ship for his Lower Firth services—from Ardrossan to Arran and on the Cumbrae service. In the winter of 1881 she was holed when she went aground near Fairlie, and she remained on the bottom for several days. She was re-engined in 1885, and in 1891 sold to the Glasgow & South Western Railway Co, which fitted new boilers. The G & SWR sold her in August 1893 to the Cardiff firm of Edwards & Robertson, John Gunn acquired her when Campbell's drove Edwards & Robertson out of business in 1895, and she came to Campbell's when Gunn in his turn went under.

Campbell's seem to have used *Scotia* in a number of roles. There is evidence that she operated to Ilfracombe and also in the upper Channel. She did not remain with them for long, however, for in 1903 she was sold to Italian owners, the Societa Napolitana di Navali a Vapore of Naples. She went out under her own steam and on arrival was re-named *Principessa Mafalda*. Later renamed *Epomoneo*, she is reported by one source to have been broken up in the 1920s, though another states that she was sunk by mine in 1914. As the ship disappears from the register after 1914, the latter fate is more likely.

SLIEVE DONARD/ALBION

Type	Steel Paddle Steamer
GRT	363 tons
Length	200.0ft
Breadth	25.0ft
Depth	8.3ft
Builders	J. & G. Thomson Ltd, Clydebank
Engine Makers	Builders
Engine Type	CD 2 cyls, 26in, 55-54in
NHP	185
Yard No	266
Speed	18 knots

Albion was built as the Belfast & County Down Railway Company's steamship *Slieve Donard*, and it was under this name that she was bought in 1899 by Captain Alexander Campbell on his own account. He operated her in the Bristol Channel during that year and in 1900 she was transferred to P. & A. Campbell Ltd with her new name *Albion*.

An 18-knot steamer, *Albion* was reputed to be a very wet ship forward, probably due to her open forecastle. She also possessed very large paddle wheels, which projected below the line of the hull, although their diameter was later reduced. The ship does not seem to have been rebuilt as completely as most Campbell acquisitions and completed her career largely as designed.

For the 1900 season she joined *Cambria* at Southampton and continued on that station during 1901 and 1902. While operating from Bournemouth on 3 May 1901 she was in collision with Cosen's *Empress* when both steamers chose the same time to back out from Bournemouth pier, though from opposite sides. *Albion* was present at both naval reviews in 1902, but returned to the Bristol Channel for the 1903 season, and was stationed at Newport.

On Easter Bank Holiday Monday 1907, under the command of Captain James Webber, she left on an excursion to Portishead and Bristol with a full load of passengers. Early morning fog covered the Channel and *Albion* touched ground in the mouth of the Usk while leaving Newport. She then sailed direct for Portishead and nothing further was seen through the fog until she came to an abrupt and grinding halt! When the crew scrambled ashore, they found *Albion* was approximately 30yd west of the Blacknore lighthouse at Portishead and firmly aground. Her passengers were brought to shore and sent on to Bristol by train, and it appears that neither they nor *Albion* were any worse for the incident. The ship floated off on the next tide, assisted by tugs from Messrs C. J. Kings.

The year 1912 found *Albion* late in the season at Brighton and she continued there in 1913 and 1914, finishing out the 1914 season even though war had been declared. She was requisitioned by the Admiralty on 1 July 1915 and fitted out for minesweeping duties. Renamed *Albyn* to avoid confusion with the battleship *Albion*, she carried out minesweeping duties while based on Dover and returned to Bristol on 15 February 1919.

Albion's condition was such after her war service that she was scrapped, but there was a sequel. The good condition of her engines led to their removal, storage at Troon and subsequent installation for further use in *Glen Gower* (see p75).

39 (*above left*) Albion *in the Avon Gorge. She retained this rig throughout her career*

40 (*below left*) Albion *aground on Black Nore Point, Portishead, 1 April 1907*

41 Bonnie Doon *in the Avon, 1910. Compare her condition here with Plate 2*

	BONNIE DOON
Type	Steel Paddle Steamer
GRT	272 tons
Length	218.0ft
Breadth	20.0ft
Depth	7.5ft
Builders	T. B. Seath & Co Ltd, Rutherglen
Engine Makers	A. Campbell & Son
Engine Type	D1 cyl, 50-72in
NHP	96
Yard No	172
Speed	14 knots

Bonnie Doon is a historic steamer—the first pleasure steamer proper to operate from Bristol, in the summer of 1886. On 22 May of that year she operated an excursion that was the forerunner of many thousands of trips by paddle steamers in the Bristol Channel. Before this venture she had been put on show at the Old Drawbridge, where over 10,000 people inspected her.

Bonnie Doon did not enter the Campbell fleet until March 1899, although for years she had been a familiar vessel to anyone associated with the company. She was built in 1876 for a Scots consortium led by her builder, T. B. Seath, for service between Glasgow and Ayr. *Bonnie Doon* was never a successful ship mechanically, and very early in her career she acquired a nickname on the Clyde of *Bonnie Breakdoon*. In 1881 she was sold to Liverpool for the Liverpool & Llandudno & Welsh Coast Steamship company. She stayed on the Mersey for one year and then returned to Scotland, to be based at Wemyss Bay under the ownership of Messrs Gillies and Campbell.

Chartered by a Bristol syndicate, she came to the Bristol Channel in May 1886, as related above, and in 1887 she was bought outright by a group of businessmen among whom the King family, owners of the present Bristol tug company, were prominent. Further changes of ownership followed in quick succession: 1889 found *Bonnie Doon* at Belfast, but she was back in 1890 in the fleet of Edwards & Robertson at Cardiff; in 1896 John Gunn, another Cardiff owner, bought her from Edwards & Robertson; and when Gunn sold out to Campbell's, *Bonnie Doon* was still one of his fleet.

It is surprising that Campbell's operated this ship as long as they did. It may be that nobody wanted her and she was possibly more profitable to operate than to sell for scrap. The only structural alteration made was a new funnel in March 1907. She spent the 5 years up to the end of the 1910 season working out of Brighton, though there is no record of her crossing the Channel.

From 1911 to 1912 *Bonnie Doon* operated in the Bristol Channel, based at Newport, and her days ended in November 1913 when the Dutch ocean-going tug *Zuider Zee* arrived at Bristol to tow her to Rotterdam for breaking up.

BRIGHTON QUEEN (I)

Type	Steel Paddle Steamer
GRT	603 tons
Length	240.5ft
Breadth	28.1ft
Depth	9.4ft
Builders	Clydebank SB & E Co Ltd
Engine Makers	Builders
Engine Type	CD 2 cyls, 30½in, 65-60in
NHP	273
Yard No	306
Speed	18 knots

Brighton Queen came from the famous Clydebank shipyard and ran her trials on 14 June 1897, before coming south to Brighton later in the same month. She was built for the Brighton, Worthing & Hove Steamship Company and immediately established a high reputation, particularly among local residents, who patronised her to the exclusion of other ships that carried 'mere holiday-makers'.

Brighton Queen was allegedly good for 20 knots throughout her career. When she came out, she had a raised forecastle, and two bridges, one forward of the funnel, with the wheelhouse, and another between the paddle boxes. Open alleyways stretched along both sides of the ship and round the saloons.

P. & A. Campbell bought out the Brighton company in November 1901 and very largely rebuilt *Brighton Queen* before putting her into service in 1902. The open alleyways were plated in, round ports were fitted and the well known cruiser pattern cowl appeared on her funnel. In fact she was the first of the Campbell fleet to be so treated, becoming the prototype from which the appearance of every other paddle steamer the company owned was derived. Even the giant *Queens* (*Bristol* and *Cardiff*—not Cunard!), constructed nearly half a century later, derived something from the style first built into the *Brighton Queen*.

Apart from an unfortunate grounding at Hastings on August Monday, 1902, *Brighton Queen* served on the south coast station without event until the outbreak of war in August 1914. Registered at Shoreham, she usually took the longer sailings from Brighton, particularly cross-Channel, and she was a frequent visitor to Calais and Boulogne. Captain John West and Captain Hector McFadyen had long periods in command of this ship.

42 (top) Brighton Queen (I) in 1897. Note her flying bridge and open alleyways

43 (above) Brighton Queen (I) as rebuilt by Campbell's. The two forward lifeboats were added after the Titanic tragedy

In 1914 she was converted at Bristol for minesweeping duties following her requisition by the Admiralty. She left Bristol on 13 September 1914 and served in the Thames Flotilla until 5 October 1915, when she struck a mine off the Belgian coast and sank.

	PRINCESS MAY
Type	Steel Paddle Steamer
GRT	260 tons
Length	160.0ft
Breadth	21.6ft
Depth	8.5ft
Builders	Barclay, Curle & Co Ltd
Engine Makers	Builders
Engine Type	CD 2 cyls, 22in, 42-42in
NHP	87
Yard No	384
Speed	12 knots

44 Princess May *at Bristol in the winter of 1901-2*

Princess May joined the Campbell fleet at the end of 1901, one of the two vessels of the Brighton, Worthing & South Coast Steam Boat Company Limited which Campbell's had bought out. Built in 1893, she was a very small steamer with an open foredeck and a saloon aft. She took her name from Princess May of Teck, who was later to become Queen Mary, wife of George V. It could be argued that this little paddle steamer preceded the great Cunard liner by at least 44 years in receiving the name of that particular Royal lady! The Brighton company used her to replace *Sea Breeze*, and she carried out a variety of services for them.

Campbell's brought her round to Bristol for refit in the following winter, and when the 1902 season opened, she appeared on the Weston-Cardiff ferry, running on Captain Alec Campbell's private account. She did not remain long in this service and it is likely that she was too small and too slow.

In the Coronation year of 1902 King Edward VII was due to review the Fleet at Spithead on 28 June. In company with *Britannia, Westward Ho, Cambria* and *Albion, Princess May* went south and ran excursions for the review. Unfortunately, King Edward was taken ill with appendicitis and the review was postponed, so *Princess May* remained at Southampton on the Cowes service, in direct competition with the Southampton Company. This arrangement was short-lived as *Princess May* caught the eye of some Italian businessmen who were in Hampshire for the naval review, and Campbell's readily agreed to her sale. She went to Italy to join the fleet of the Societa di Navigazione a Vapore della Penisola Sorrentina of Castellamare, and was renamed *Principessa Yolanda*. In 1911 she was bought by a Russian firm, Serafina Bros, for service as a tender at Odessa. Renamed *Vasilieff*, she appeared in the Register until 1930.

	BARRY/WAVERLEY (II)
Type	Steel Paddle Steamer
GRT	471 tons
Length	225.5ft
Breadth	26.6ft
Depth	8.7ft
Builders	J. Brown & Co Ltd, Clydebank
Engine Makers	Builders
Engine Type	CD 2 cyls, 25½in, 54-54in
NHP	178
Yard No	379
Speed	17.5 knots

Barry was the second of the three ships that Campbell's acquired when they took over Bristol Channel Passenger Boats Ltd in December 1911. She had been launched on 4 May 1907 by Miss Forrest, daughter of a director of the Barry Railway Company. She was registered at Cardiff and carried the arms of Barry on her paddle boxes until they were removed in 1926. She served on the runs from Barry to Minehead and Weston for the BCPB company, and continued to do much the same work when taken over by Campbell's.

Barry's service in World War I was prodigious. After transferring numbers of German prisoners from the SS *Trevilley* and taking them from Bristol to Dublin in 1914, then moving internees from Dublin to the Isle of Man, she was sent in July 1915 to join the Mediterranean fleet in support of the Gallipoli operation. In the Aegean she performed all manner of services and is reputed to have been the last ship out of Suvla Bay when that ill fated position was abandoned on 9 January 1916. She remained in Greek waters, based on Salonika, where her name was changed to *Barryfield* during 1917 to avoid confusion with an American destroyer serving in the same waters.

Barry returned in 1919, and was thoroughly reconditioned by the Ailsa company at Troon in 1920. In 1926 she was renamed *Waverley*, given a small refit and then transferred to the Brighton station, where she remained for the rest of her career except for the seasons of

45 (*above left*) Barry *running her trials in 1907. Built for the Barry Railway Company, she eventually became Campbell's second* Waverley

46 (*below left*) Barry *in White Funnel colours as* Waverley (II)

1934 and 1935. A bow rudder was fitted in 1934.

September 1939 saw *Barry* called up again, this time with her fourth name, HMS *Snaefell*. After conversion to a minesweeper at Milford Haven she joined the east coast flotillas and played a heroine's part in the Dunkirk operations when she rescued *Glen Gower*, aground and helpless, under German artillery fire.

The career of this active little ship ended on 5 July 1941, when she was caught by German bombers outside Sunderland and sunk.

DEVONIA (I)

Type	Steel Paddle Steamer
GRT	641 tons
Length	245.0ft
Breadth	29.0ft
Depth	9.7ft
Builders	J. Brown & Co Ltd, Clydebank
Engine Makers	Builders
Engine Type	CD 2 cyls, $34\frac{1}{2}$in, 71-60in
NHP	325
Yard No	369
Speed	19 knots

47 (left) *Full out,* Devonia *adds to a murky Clyde day when running trials in 1905*

48 (top) Devonia *in Red Funnel colours about 1909*

49 (above) Devonia *at Newhaven in 1930. A stump mainmast has been added and two forward lifeboats*

This lovely steamer entered the Campbell fleet in December 1911 together with *Barry* and *Westonia*, following the demise of Bristol Channel Passenger Boats Ltd. She was launched on 22 March 1905 by Mrs Radford, wife of a director of the Barry Railway Company, and attained 20.5 knots on her trials. The arms of the City of Cardiff appeared on her paddle boxes and she was registered at that port. *Devonia* remained in her original condition for much of her career, the only noticeable structural alterations being the fitting of naval cowls to the funnels in 1912, and the addition of two new lifeboats in 1938. A wireless installation caused the erection of a stump mainmast after World War I. Campbell's used the ship in the Bristol Channel until 1914, when, like all the other vessels in the fleet, *Devonia* was called up as a minesweeper. She left Bristol at the end of September for Devonport and spent the war on the east coast, where she gained a reputation among minesweeping experts as the best vessel for this kind of service. She returned to Bristol in May 1919 and was refitted. She came out in 1920 on the Cardiff-Ilfracombe run and stayed there until the 1923 season, when she went to the Brighton station for 10 years. On the south coast she usually made the long trips to Boulogne, Calais, Ramsgate and Margate. Re-registered at Bristol in 1932, she was back in the Bristol Channel in 1933, where she served until 1938 and then laid up for the 1939 season.

After fitting out as a minesweeper at Milford Haven in the early part of 1939, *Devonia* served on the east coast of Scotland until the Dunkirk operation. There she was strafed by the Luftwaffe and abandoned on the beach at Lapanne, on 31 May 1940. Several photographs show her in this condition, and since then persistent stories have been told of her repair by the Germans and her continued existence in Germany to this day. The historical section of the German Ministry of Defence and the German War Museum authorities at Stuttgart have carried out considerable research on behalf of the present author to prove or disprove this story. All the French and Belgian records of the day were destroyed during the war and the main existing source is the War Diary of the German Harbour Commandant appointed to take over Dunkirk. He makes no reference to *Devonia* at all, but he does say that several small ships beached were broken up for scrap in the winter of 1940-41 and it is likely that *Devonia* was one of these.

WESTONIA/TINTERN

Type	Steel Paddle Steamer
GRT	393 tons
Length	210.1ft
Breadth	25.1ft
Depth	8.4ft
Builders	J. Scott & Co Ltd, Kinghorn
Engine Makers	Builders
Engine Type	CD 2 cyls, 27in, 58-54in
NHP	206
Yard No	106
Speed	16.5 knots

When one considers that this much renamed and resold ship was built as late as 1889, her design was curiously old fashioned. As built, her bridge was aft of the two funnels and open alleyways were fitted. She was built as *Tantallon Castle* for the Galloway Steam Packet Company, and it was proposed to use her for the excursion traffic in south-west Scotland. However, in 1901 she was sold to a Captain Lee for service at Brighton and given the name *Sussex Belle*. Captain Lee was absorbed into the Sussex Steam Packet Company, but this arrangement only lasted until the end of 1902, and the ship was sold for operations in 1903 to the Colwyn Bay & Liverpool Steamship Company.

Yet another new name, *Rhos Colwyn*, followed but within 2 years the vessel had been sold again, this time to the Barry Railway Company in South Wales. Here she remained at least for the next 6 years, mainly on the Cardiff-Weston route, while the Barry Rail-

50 (*above right*) Westonia *heading a Campbell paddler into Bristol*

51 (*right*) *The rebuilt* Westonia *came out as* Tintern. *Photographs of* Tintern *are rare. Contrast this with Plate 50*

way Company changed the name of its steamship operations three times to meet legal requirements. In 1900 she had been fitted with a very ugly forecastle and this was removed during her years at Barry. The BRC called the ship *Westonia*, but she appears to have had two more owners before being taken over by P. & A. Campbell in December 1911, together with *Devonia* and *Barry*.

Westonia was completely rebuilt by Campbell's and her appearance altered to fit the image of the White Funnel Fleet. She was reboiled, and the two original funnels were replaced by one with the standard naval cowl fitted. The open alleyways were plated up and round portholes were fitted. When she emerged for the 1912 season, she looked a typical Campbell vessel and was given the name *Tintern*.

Tintern was reputedly a very wet ship forward, due to low freeboard at the bow. Campbell's operated her for the 1912 season only and then sold her in May 1913 to the South & South Western Railway of Portugal for their ferry service across the Tagus at Lisbon. She was renamed *Alentjo* and served until 1929.

LADY ISMAY	
Type	Steel Paddle Steamer
GRT	495 tons
Length	220.0ft
Breadth	26.1ft
Depth	8.8ft
Builders	Ailsa SB Co Ltd, Troon
Engine Makers	Builders
Engine Type	CD 2 cyls, 26½in, 52-54in
NHP	115
Yard No	234
Speed	17.5 knots

52 Lady Ismay *coming down the Avon at Bristol. The main A4 road now runs along the towpath in the background*

At the end of the 1910 season the company ordered its first new steamer on its own account since the *Britannia* joined the fleet in 1896. An order was placed with the Ailsa Company at Troon, which led to a successful

daughter, would perform the ceremony, and there appears to be no record why the last minute switch of sponsors occurred. The name is unusual. Lady Ismay was a daughter of Lady Creighton Davies.

Lady Ismay is said to have been designed for the Cardiff-Weston ferry, and was indeed registered at Cardiff, although the company announced that they intended to use her for cross-Channel excursions to France. But they never did and she spent her entire service in the Bristol Channel.

Lady Ismay was powered by direct acting diagonal compound engines and was a typical specimen of the British 'standard' paddle steamer. Flush-decked, she had saloon portholes from the start of her career, and numerous vessels copied her appearance. The company claimed a speed of $17\frac{1}{2}$ knots but 15 is a more likely figure, which was adequate for the Cardiff-Weston run, on which she carried over 1,000 passengers when full.

Lady Ismay was requisitioned by the Royal Navy for war service on 2 December 1914 and fitted out as a minesweeper. She joined the Grimsby Flotilla, and while minesweeping in the Thames Estuary on 21 December 1915, she struck a mine near the Longsand Light vessel and sank almost immediately.

collaboration between the two firms and the production of several outstanding steamers. The new ship was launched on 1 June 1911 and named *Lady Ismay* by Mrs Hugh Highgate of Blairmoor House. The Bristol papers in the previous week had announced that Miss Nellie Campbell, Captain Peter Campbell's

	GLEN AVON
Type	Steel Paddle Steamer
GRT	509 tons
Length	220.0ft
Breadth	27.1ft
Depth	8.9ft
Builders	Ailsa SB Co Ltd, Troon
Engine Makers	Builders
Engine Type	CD 2 cyls, $26\frac{1}{2}$in, 52-54in
NHP	165
Yard No	225
Speed	17.5 knots

53 (*above*) *The trim* Glen Avon *off Weston-super-Mare. She retained this appearance throughout her civilian career*

54 (*below*) Glen Avon *returning from war service in 1919*

55 (*above*) Glen Avon's *port paddle-box, 25 May 1939*

55a (*below*) Glen Avon *as an AA ship in 1942*

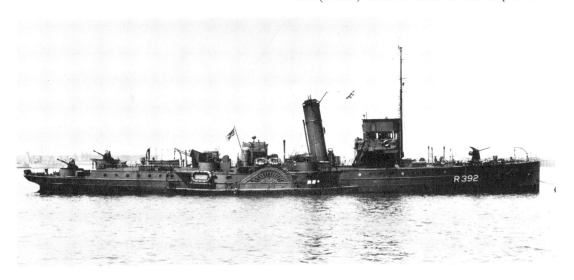

Glen Avon was a slightly larger version of *Lady Ismay*, and a ship designed for economy rather than high-speed runs. A large payload was carried and the ship was specially designed for operations in the upper Bristol Channel. She was launched from the Ailsa Company's yard on 30 May 1912, and this time Miss Nellie Campbell did indeed perform the naming ceremony. It was always said that *Glen Avon* was registered at Newport with the object of increasing trade from that town, but the 1914 register gives Bristol as her port of registry, and she carried a picture of the Avon Gorge on her paddle boxes.

Called up into the Royal Navy on 2 December 1914, she served as a minesweeper until March 1919, when she returned to the Bristol Channel, serving there throughout the inter-war period. Her wartime adventures make more interesting reading than her rather routine peacetime duties. On 15 August 1915, in company with three other Campbell steamers, she was in action with a U-boat in the North Sea, and in early April 1916 she was involved with *Westward Ho* in salvaging a wrecked Zeppelin airship.

She became well known on the Cardiff-Minehead run, and occasionally worked local excursions from Ilfracombe to Clovelly. During World War I she was fully fitted with a mainmast, but this was removed when she returned to civilian work. On 13 September 1939 *Glen Avon* was recalled to the Navy and again designated as a minesweeper. After fitting out at Milford Haven, she joined the 8th Minesweeping Flotilla on the east coast and served in the evacuation of Dunkirk. In 1942 she became an auxiliary anti-aircraft ship and went south in 1944 for the Normandy Landings. While serving off the French coast on 2 September 1944 near Port-en-Bessin, she was caught in a gale and sank.

GLEN USK

Type	Steel Paddle Steamer
GRT	524 tons
Length	224.3ft
Breadth	28.1ft
Depth	8.9ft
Builders	Ailsa SB Co Ltd, Troon
Engine Makers	Builders
Engine Type	CD 2 cyls, 26½in, 52-54in
NHP	165
Yard No	187
Speed	17.5 knots

56 Glen Usk *at Hotwells pontoon in 1914*

The last steamer to be built for the company before World War I, *Glen Usk* was launched on 11 April 1914 by Mrs Peter Campbell. The ship was ordered specifically for the Newport trade and was registered in that port; a picture of Newport Castle appeared on her paddle boxes. Despite the awful lesson of the *Titanic*, the *Western Daily Press* the day after the launch announced that the new steamer was 'practically unsinkable'. It went on to add enthusiastically that *Glen Usk* would be 'furnished in the most tasteful and luxurious manner'. A good looking steamer, *Glen Usk* performed useful work throughout her career,

which had hardly started before she was called up for service in the Royal Navy. She left Bristol in February 1915 in company with *Britannia* and spent the war in Scots waters. The success of these small ships as mine-sweepers was so outstanding that the *Glen Usk* design became the prototype for the *Ascot* class paddle minesweepers which were built from 1915 onwards. Some of these eventually became pleasure steamers in their own right.

Glen Usk served as a minesweeping flotilla leader, and as such appeared at the surrender of the German High Seas Fleet in November 1918. Following the war she was given the

57 (*above left*) *The well worn port paddle-box of* Glen Usk *in her last year*

58 (*left*) Cymru am byth! Glen Usk *using a Welsh ensign at her jack staff after the White Funnel move to Cardiff in 1956*

59 (*above*) *Everybody down! Passengers being put ashore after* Glen Usk *grounded in the Avon, 30 August 1959*

characteristic 'jigger' mainmast and continued operating in the Bristol Channel, mostly from Newport or Swansea. In 1933 she was re-registered at Bristol. She went south to Spithead for the Coronation Naval Review of May 1937.

Called up for service again in September 1939, she fitted out at Penarth and then went round to the east coast on minesweeping duties. She missed the Dunkirk operation be-

74

cause she was under repair at the time. In early 1942 she was converted to an anti-aircraft ship and went to the south coast for the Normandy landings. Early in 1945 she was chartered to the Dutch Government and spent several months in the Netherlands on relief work in the Rotterdam area.

Her second span of war service ended in October 1945, and she was refitted at Bristol. Her first postwar sailing was on 24 July 1946, and she continued to operate in the Bristol Channel until the Coronation Review of 1953 took her on a visit to the south coast. In 1954 she received a full mainmast and gaff. *Glen Usk* was laid up for the 1957 season, as passenger traffic in the Bristol Channel dwindled, but she was out again in 1958. In 1959 she made the headlines in a big way when on 30 August she went aground in the Horseshoe Bend of the River Avon, outward bound for Clevedon, Penarth and Cardiff with more than

600 passengers on board. The ship stuck fast and the passengers were led ashore, some collecting a little of the notorious Avon mud on the way. One gentleman is reported to have appeared on deck dressed only in his vest and underpants! *Glen Usk* was refloated on the next tide by the tugs *Bristolian* and *John King* and was reported undamaged after inspection at Avonmouth. The seasons of 1961 and 1962 saw the ship laid up again, and on 29 April 1963 she was towed from Penarth en route for Cork for breaking up at Passage West.

DUCHESS OF DEVONSHIRE

Type	Steel Paddle Steamer
GRT	221 tons
Length	170.0ft
Breadth	20.4ft
Depth	8.1ft
Builders	R. & H. Green, Blackwall
Engine Makers	John Penn, Greenwich
Engine Type	Compound diagonal 2 cyl
NHP	101
Yard No	614
Speed	12 knots

60 *A historic photograph of* Duchess of Devonshire *in White Funnel colours on the Weston-Cardiff ferry in World War I*

With its entire fleet requisitioned for war service, the Campbell company was forced to charter tonnage in the years 1917-19 in order to work skeleton services in the Upper Bristol Channel. The vessel concerned was the Devon Dock, Pier & Steamship Company's *Duchess of Devonshire*. She appeared on the Cardiff-Weston ferry in 1917, crewed by a number of retired Campbell employees, and her officers' list contained at least four ex-captains.

Duchess of Devonshire was built for the old Devon Steamship Company in 1892, and designed to nose on to the beaches of West Bay and Lyme Bay. She was a regular visitor from Torquay to Sidmouth, Seaton and Bridport, and occasionally went east to Weymouth or as far afield as the Solent, where she appeared for the 1897 Diamond Jubilee Review.

Campbell's used her again in 1918 and 1919 (during which year she spent the latter part of the season stationed at Newport). She then returned to her Torquay services in 1920, and continued operations for 10 years, until she was laid up in 1930. The West Bay steamer trade was virtually at an end, as Campbell's

were to find from their ill fated efforts with *Westward Ho* in 1932; nonetheless *Duchess of Devonshire* was bought in 1933 for further operations by the South Devon & West Bay Steamship Company. But her new owners had little service out of her, for her end came on 27 August 1934 at Sidmouth. She had nosed on to the beach and landed passengers over the bow as usual, an operation always carried out by dropping a stern anchor—but on this occasion the anchor dragged. The ship was wrecked broadside on to Sidmouth beach, from which she never came off, and she was broken up *in situ*.

	GLEN GOWER
Type	Steel Paddle Steamer
GRT	553 tons
Length	235.1ft
Breadth	28.5ft
Depth	9.1ft
Builders	Ailsa SB Co Ltd, Troon
Engine Makers	J. & G. Thomson Ltd, Clydebank
Engine Type	CD 2 cyls, 26in, 55-54in
NHP	184
Yard No	377
Speed	16.5 knots

When *Albion* was scrapped in 1919, her engines were removed (see p55) because a survey showed them to be capable of further use; but it was not until 14 February 1922 that the steamer for which they were intended was launched and named by Mrs Alec Campbell. The new ship was *Glen Gower*, and Campbell's ordered her specially for the Swansea station, in which port she was registered. In appearance the new paddler was a typical Ailsa product, with flush deck and round ports, though her 235ft length made her the longest ship built to date specifically for

61 (*above*) Glen Gower *in her last years of service*

61a (*below*) Glen Gower *as HMS* Glenmore *in 1942*

62 Mumbles lighthouse is depicted on Glen Gower's *paddle boxes, 6 May 1934*

Campbell's. The acquisitions *Devonia* and *Lady Moyra* were, of course, longer by some 10ft. When she first came out, *Glen Gower* carried the small after 'jigger' mast that was a prominent feature of all the steamers between the wars. In 1954 she was given a full mainmast and gaff, which greatly enhanced her appearance. It is a matter for speculation whether *Glen Gower* would have been built at all if the two paddlers of the Yellow Funnel Line had come on the market earlier than they did. However, the announcement that *Lady Moyra* and *Lady Evelyn* were for sale was not made until the day after the maiden voyage of *Glen Gower* from Bristol on 2 June 1922, when she ran a cheap afternoon trip to Ilfracombe. Bristol passengers returned in the *Britannia* while *Glen Gower* went on to Swansea to take up her duties.

Swansea was her home port until the early 1930s, although she did spend part of the 1926 season at Brighton. In 1932 she made a voyage to Dublin on charter. In 1934, however, she went permanently to the south coast and served there until the outbreak of war. On this station she usually undertook the local work, but made frequent cross-Channel trips to Boulogne from Eastbourne and Hastings. In 1937 she was present at the Coronation Naval Review.

Glen Gower's war service started on 15 September 1939, when she was renamed *Glenmore*. Following conversion to a mine-sweeper, the ship joined the 8th Minesweeping Flotilla and served on the east coast. *Glen Gower* was present at Dunkirk in 1940 and the official war records show she evacuated 1,235 men from that port. During the operation she went aground near Lapanne and came under fire from German artillery. She suffered twelve casualties dead before being towed away by another Campbell steamer, *Waverley*. During the latter part of the war she served at Harwich on coastal convoy duty, and she operated in Belgian waters following the liberation of Antwerp. She arrived back in Bristol from the Belgian port on 25 June 1945 and underwent a lengthy refit, emerging for the 1947 season. *Glen Gower* returned to the south coast in company with *Empress Queen*, and spent a number of seasons there in the late 1940s and early 1950s. She attended her second Coronation Review on 15 June 1953.

Glen Gower ran the company's first post-war cross-Channel trips in July 1954, but the south coast trade never recovered its prewar profitability, and the final trips from Brighton were made at the end of the 1956 season. The ship ran in the 1957 season on the Bristol Channel but was laid up in 1958 and never sailed commercially again. She left Penarth under tow on 7 April 1960, to be scrapped in Belgium.

LADY EVELYN / BRIGHTON BELLE

Type	Steel Paddle Steamer
GRT	320 tons
Length	200.0ft
Breadth	24.1ft
Depth	8.2ft
Builders	J. Scott & Co Ltd, Kinghorn
Engine Makers	Builders
Engine Type	CD 2 cyls, 22in, 48-54in
NHP	141
Yard No	110
Speed	13 knots

Campbell's bought *Lady Evelyn*, together with *Lady Moyra*, when the mortgagees of Tucker's Yellow Funnel Fleet offered both vessels for sale in June 1922. Somewhat smaller than her contemporaries, *Lady Evelyn* was launched in 1900 for the Furness Railway Company and used by them for their Lake District excursions on the Fleetwood, Morecambe and Barrow services. Evidently she proved too small for this traffic because she was lengthened by Vickers' at Barrow in 1904 by some 30ft.

After service in World War I as a mine-sweeper at Larne in Northern Ireland, *Lady Evelyn* came to the Bristol Channel in 1920 when Tucker's bought her.

Campbell's made several alterations to the ship, particularly to the funnel and bridge, and added a mainmast. They also changed her name to *Brighton Belle* before sending her to her name port in 1923. She was fitted with round portholes in 1924.

Brighton Belle served on the south coast until the 1936 season, when she returned to the Bristol Channel. Vickers' at Barrow re-boilered her in 1934 with a secondhand boiler, and in 1937 her hull was painted grey temporarily, an experiment fortunately not repeated.

63 (top) *The pretty little* Brighton Belle

64 (above) Brighton Belle *in cruising grey. The experiment was not considered a success*

At the outbreak of World War II *Brighton Belle* fitted out at Penarth and then served at North Shields until the Dunkirk operation, where she rescued 800 men on her first sortie. But, when returning to the beaches, she struck sunken wreckage in the Downs and was heavily damaged. Attempts to tow her to safety failed and she sank on 28 May 1940, her crew being taken off by the paddle steamer *Medway Queen.*

LADY MOYRA/BRIGHTON QUEEN (II)

Type	Steel Paddle Steamer
GRT	519 tons
Length	245.0ft
Breadth	29.0ft
Depth	9.7ft
Builders	J. Brown & Co Ltd, Clydebank
Engine Makers	Builders
Engine Type	CD, 2 cyls, 24½in, 71-60in
NHP	325
Yard No	368
Speed	18.5 knots

This sister of *Devonia* was launched from the same yard on 24 February 1905 by Mrs Forrest, and named *Gwalia*. The ship had a somewhat mixed early career. She was first registered at Cardiff, but was sold in 1910 by the Barry Railway Company to the Furness Railway Company, which renamed her *Lady Moyra* and set her to work on their Fleetwood, Morecambe and Barrow services. After war service as a minesweeper in the Portland Flotilla, *Lady Moyra* was sold to the Yellow Funnel Fleet of W. H. Tucker & Company Ltd at Cardiff; but that company went out of business in early 1922 and *Lady Moyra*, together with *Lady Evelyn*, was offered for auction on the Baltic Exchange on 3 June of that year. Both ships were bought by P. & A. Campbell Ltd.

Lady Moyra served in the Bristol Channel until 1932, when she was re-registered at Bristol and renamed *Brighton Queen*. Her transfer to the south coast for the 1933 season

65 *(above right)* Gwalia *on trials in 1905*

66 *(right) The stately* Lady Moyra *arriving at Ilfracombe. She became* Brighton Queen (II)

followed, and she stayed on the Brighton station for the rest of her civilian career. A bow rudder was fitted in 1934, presumably to help with manoeuvring in the confined entrances to French harbours such as Calais, Boulogne, Fécamp and Trouville, where she was a frequent visitor.

Brighton Queen was converted to a minesweeper at Milford Haven on the outbreak of World War II and served on the east coast of Scotland until the Dunkirk operation. While returning from the French port with 700 troops on board on 31 May 1940, she was struck and sunk by German bombers with heavy loss of life, although all the Bristol crew on board were rescued.

DUKE OF DEVONSHIRE

Type	Steel Paddle Steamer
GRT	257 tons
Length	175.0ft
Breadth	20.6ft
Depth	8.2ft
Builders	R. & H. Green Ltd, London
Engine Makers	J. Penn & Son Ltd, London
Engine Type	CD 2 cyls, 23in, 46-36in
NHP	106
Yard No	None allotted
Speed	12.5 knots

Duke of Devonshire was bought from the Devon Dock, Pier & Steam Ship Company Ltd in 1933. She had been delivered in 1896 and was destined for a long life. Like her half-sister, *Duchess of Devonshire*, she was built with a shallow draught forward in order that she could nose on to the beaches at such places as Sidmouth, Seaton and Bridport (West Bay). She spent all her career on the south coast and, while in Devon ownership, went as far afield as Spithead for naval reviews. During World

67 *An early picture of* Duke of Devonshire

War I, *Duke of Devonshire* set up a record for paddle steamers on war service: converted for minesweeping duties, she served at Gallipoli, traversed the Suez Canal and sailed in the Persian Gulf before returning to the United Kingdom—all under her own steam.

The *Duke* continued her excursions from Torquay after World War I, but increasing competition, which culminated with the arrival of Campbell's *Westward Ho* at Torquay and Plymouth in 1932, led to the withdrawal of the Devon company's larger ships. Campbell's bought *Duke of Devonshire* in 1933, but did not run her—it seems the purchase was purely to buy up a prospective competitor—and the little ship was promptly sold to a Cork operator, Jeremiah Dwyer, who ran her from the

Irish port until July 1936, when she returned to Torquay. Her Torquay owner, Alexander Taylor, sold her in his turn to the Weymouth company of Cosens & Co in the spring of 1938.

Cosens' renamed her *Consul* and she ran for them until 1963. After World War II, in which she served as a naval examination vessel, she was converted to burn oil fuel and received the last of a number of refits that had considerably altered her appearance from the days when she was built. Sold to South Coast & Continental Steamers, she appeared at Hastings and Eastbourne in 1963, but was back at Weymouth in 1964, where she proved unprofitable. Sold as a floating hostel in the River Dart at the end of that year, she reverted to her original name. She was eventually sold for breaking up on the Itchen at Southampton in 1968.

	EMPRESS QUEEN
Type	Steel Twin Screw Ship
GRT	1,781 tons
Length	269.5ft
Breadth	37.5ft
Depth	12.0ft
Builders	Ailsa SB Co Ltd, Troon
Engine Makers	Harland & Wolff Ltd, Belfast
Engine Type	4 st turbs, SRG
NHP	650
Yard No	430
Speed	20 knots

Campbell's announced the impending construction of the *Empress Queen* in the Bristol newspapers on 17 February 1939, and the

68 *The first screw-driven Campbell steamer,* Empress Queen

details came as a shock to the traditionalists. Not only was the new vessel to be the largest ever built for the company, but she was to be screw-driven! Campbell's intention in building her was to exploit day trips to France from the south coast resorts of Brighton, Eastbourne and Hastings, and she was thus designed to carry 2,000 passengers at a cruising speed of 20 knots. War broke out before the ship could be completed. She was launched and named by Mrs Banks on 29 February 1940 and taken over by the Admiralty on 4 July of the same year. Renamed *Queen Eagle* to avoid confusion with the Scottish paddle steamer *Empress Queen*, the new vessel became an anti-aircraft ship in the Thames Estuary. In November 1943 she was released to the Ministry of War Transport, her original name was restored and she went on the Stranraer-

69 Empress Queen *on war service as* HMS Queen Eagle

Larne ferry, where she remained until October 1946.

Reconditioned by her builders, *Empress Queen* arrived in Bristol for the first time on 18 June 1947, the day before *Cardiff Queen* arrived from the Clyde.

Now began a series of unsatisfactory seasons on the south coast. Her designed role of running cross-Channel excursions was denied to *Empress Queen* because of British Government currency regulations, and so this huge steamer was forced to carry out coastal excursions for which she proved too large to operate or fill. She ran from Brighton from 1947 to 1950 and then was switched to Torquay in 1951 in an attempt to run day trips to the Channel Islands. The experiment was not successful and *Empress Queen* was laid up

at Narrow Quay, Bristol, for the 1952 season. In 1953 she was advertised for sale.

Empress Queen was bought in the spring of 1955 by the Kavounides Brothers of the Piraeus, Greece, and renamed *Phillipos*. She left Bristol under her own steam on 3 April 1955. The Greek company extensively rebuilt her and converted her machinery to diesel power.

On 26 February 1972, while the ship was being prepared for the coming season, an accident to welding equipment caused a fire that rapidly got out of control. *Phillipos* was berthed in the centre of a group of ships at the time and she became a danger to those lying alongside her. She was therefore towed away and beached nearby where she was allowed to burn out. Refloated, she was berthed at Ambelaki and was still there in December 1972, awaiting a decision on her future use.

	BRISTOL QUEEN
Type	Steel Paddle Steamer
GRT	961 tons
Length	258.5ft
Breadth	31.2ft
Depth	10.5ft
Builders	Chas Hill & Sons Ltd, Bristol
Engine Makers	Rankin & Blackmore Ltd
Engine Type	TD 3 cyls, 27in, 42in, 66-66in
Shaft HP	2,700
Yard No	334
Speed	18 knots

Bristol Queen was the first steamer to be

70 Bristol Queen *in 1965*

built for the company following the end of World War II. She was notable in being the first ship that Campbell's ordered from a yard in their home port, rather than from Scotland, and the first to be named after Bristol. The vessel was launched on 4 April 1946 by Mrs John Owen, then Lady Mayoress of Bristol. At the launch there was a curious repetition of history when, as with the *Great Britain* over a century previously, two attempts were necessary in order to smash the bottle against her side before she would move down the slips! In this case it was a bottle of 'Bristol Milk', the well known brand of sherry. The local press also reported, with some pride, that Peter Cambell's two sons were present at the launch.

71 *A striking shot of the powerful* Bristol Queen *in the Avon*

Bristol Queen went into service in the following summer, running her trials in the Bristol Channel on 7 September 1946. Her maiden voyage followed on 14 September.

This ship represents the final development of the pleasure excursion steamer in the British Isles. She was the largest paddle steamer built for Campbell's, with a powerful set of triple expansion engines. Oil-fired boilers gave her a service speed of 18 knots, though she is reputed to have exceeded 20 knots on certain occasions—once when she raced the Swedish-America liner *Kungsholm* down the Bristol Channel from Walton Bay.

Since a number of Bristol Channel piers remained under military control at the end of the war, *Bristol Queen* did not settle down to her intended routes until the early 1950s, but then she was generally employed on the longer runs from the Upper Bristol Channel ports to Ilfracombe and Lundy. She was present at the Coronation Naval Review on 15 June 1953. When the company was in serious financial difficulties at the end of the 1950s, she was laid up in Penarth Dock for the whole of the 1959 and 1960 seasons, but came out again in 1961.

In 1963 she inaugurated the annual three-day trip to Penzance and the Scilly Isles, leaving on 17 May. These trips have proved successful and have been repeated by various vessels annually since then.

CARDIFF QUEEN	
Type	Steel Paddle Steamer
GRT	765 tons
Length	240.0ft
Breadth	30.1ft
Depth	9.75ft
Builders	Fairfield SB & E Co Ltd
Engine Makers	Builders
Engine Type	TD 3 cyls, 25½in, 39in, 61-60in
NHP	332
Yard No	738
Speed	17.5 knots

When *Cardiff Queen* was withdrawn from service at the end of the 1966 season, most enthusiasts thought that *Bristol Queen* would be with them for at least a few more years. It was not to be, however. On 28 August 1967 the ship struck a submerged object off Barry and lost a paddle blade and arm from the starboard wheel. Three days later she was taken out of service and laid up at Cardiff. In September of the same year it was announced that she was for sale.

There followed an attempt to preserve the ship as a permanent museum in Bristol's floating harbour, but this came to nothing, and she was finally sold to Belgian shipbreakers. She left Cardiff on 22 March 1968, under tow by the German tug *Fairplay XI*, and arrived at Ostend on 25 March.

For the last paddle steamer to be built for the company, P. & A. Campbell Ltd returned to the Clyde, traditional birthplace of their ships. *Cardiff Queen* was launched from the Govan Yard of Fairfield's on 26 February 1947 and named by Mrs W. J. Banks, wife of the then managing director of the company. *Cardiff Queen* arrived in Bristol for the first time on 19 June 1947, the day after *Empress Queen*'s first visit to the port. *Bristol Queen* was also in Bristol at the same time, and local people, seeing these three new large steamers all together, must indeed have thought the company's fortunes were fully restored.

Cardiff Queen spent her career largely in the shadow of her larger sister, and due to the increasing financial difficulties of the company and reduction in trade during the 1950s and 1960s, was not employed on the runs for which she was designed until the last years of her career, when the Swansea station proved to be the more economic of the company's activities. Inevitably, she spent much time on the Cardiff-Weston ferry.

She went south to Brighton for the 1952 season, reopening Campbell services from that resort following the dead season of 1951. She was present at the Coronation Review of the

72 (top) *The brand new* Cardiff Queen *on her trials in 1947*

73 (above) Cardiff Queen *landing passengers at Clovelly, 14 September 1965*

Fleet at Spithead on 15 June 1953 and remained on the south coast for the rest of the season. She was back in the Bristol Channel for 1954, where she remained for the rest of her career.

Cardiff Queen made her last commercial voyage on 21 September 1966, when, in perfect weather, she took 400 passengers to Lundy. She was then laid up in Cardiff Docks. The 1966 season had been anything but trouble-free, and the ever-rising cost of repairs made the withdrawal of the two big paddlers inevitable. In any case, the purchase of the motor vessel *Westward Ho* (ex-*Vecta*) from the Red Funnel Company at Southampton was also a sign of things to come.

It was no great surprise, therefore, when *Cardiff Queen* was put up for sale in September 1966. The usual desultory spate of proposals for future use followed. One of these was interesting in that it envisaged her use on the Firth of Forth. Nothing came of these ideas, however, though her ultimate fate was rather bizarre.

In January 1968 she was sold to Critchcraft Ltd of Chepstow, which firm proposed to use her as a floating nightclub at Newport. She arrived in that town on 29 February and was moored at Mill Parade Wharf. The infamous Bristol Channel tide now took a hand, and, as the waters receded, it was noticed that *Cardiff Queen* was sliding down the mud from the quay. She soon went aground at an astonishing angle! However, she was recovered on the next tide and taken into Newport docks. This incident, which proved fairly costly, discouraged her new owners and she was sold to shipbreakers John Cashmore Ltd, and moved to their yard for demolition on 9 April 1968.

CRESTED EAGLE	
Type	Twin-screw Motor Vessel, Steel-built
GRT	245 tons
Length	137.8ft
Breadth	25.2ft
Depth	9.0ft
Builders	J. Crown & Sons Ltd, Sunderland
Engine Makers	Crossley Bros Ltd
Engine Type	Two diesels, 6 cyl
Brake HP	330
Yard No	192
Speed	14 knots on trials (1938)

P. & A. Campbell Ltd chartered this small motor vessel from the General Steam Navigation Company Ltd for operations on the south coast in the 1957 season, the last occasion on which the company attempted to operate traditional excursion services for a full season from the south coast resorts. The ship was built before World War II as *New Royal Lady* for a private operator, Thomas Round, for operations out of Scarborough with 420 passengers. After the war she operated as far afield as the Forth. She was bought by the General Steam Navigation Company in 1947 for excursion work in the Thames, and her name was changed from *New Royal Lady* to *Crested Eagle*.

She appeared at Eastbourne in 1957 and operated mainly from that port and Hastings, with a weekly visit to Brighton. As originally built, the ship had two funnels, but the forward one was removed by GSN to give more deck space. Already an ugly ship, this alteration made her look hideous, and matters were not improved by the traditional white funnel being defaced with the Campbell house flag.

The 1957 season was notorious for bad weather on the south coast and the ship spent much time lying up in Newhaven. The whole charter scheme was a financial failure, and at the end of 1957 it was announced that Campbell's would not be operating in the area in 1958. At the same time the General Steam Navigation Company sold *Crested Eagle* to Messrs E. Zammit & E. Magro of Malta, GC, and she was still operating in October 1971 as Magro Brothers motor vessel *Imperial Eagle* between Malta and Gozo.

74 Crested Eagle *in her Maltese role as* Imperial Eagle

75 St Trillo *at Birnbeck Pier, Weston, on 13 October 1963. Campbell's owned the pier until August 1972, when it was sold for use as an entertainment centre*

	ST TRILLO
Type	Steel Twin-screw Motor Vessel
GRT	314 tons
Length	149.2ft
Breadth	27.1ft
Depth	10.0ft
Builders	Fairfield SB & E Co Ltd
Engine Makers	Crossley Bros
Engine Type	2 SCSA 12 cyls, 10-13½in
NHP	232
Yard No	657
Speed	12 knots

Excursion enthusiasts in the Bristol Channel were delighted when it was announced in 1963 that this pretty little motor vessel had been acquired by George Nott Industries and placed on charter to P. & A. Campbell Ltd. Her registered owners were Townsend Ferries—a Nott subsidiary.

St Trillo, which started life as *St Silio,* was built in 1936 and launched on 24 March of that year for the Liverpool & North Wales Steam Ship Company. She was built for local cruises and excursions from Llandudno, and was used for that purpose for the whole of her career with the Liverpool company. Before World War II she used to visit some of the smaller Anglesey ports, such as Cemaes Bay on the north coast of the island.

During the war *St Silio* was requisitioned and started duties in November 1939 as an examination vessel at Liverpool. She stayed there until February 1945, when she spent eight months as a tender to troopships on the Clyde. She was renamed *St Trillo* in November 1945. In November 1962 the Liverpool & North Wales Steam Ship Company went into liquidation, and *St Trillo* arrived at Cardiff on 13 March 1963 to take up her work for P. & A. Campbell Ltd. She opened the company's operations in the Bristol Channel for the 1963 season and then returned to Llandudno, where she served until the end of the 1969 season.

St Trillo made some extraordinary trips in the Bristol Channel, where Campbell's sometimes used her to open or close the season. She made an attempt to reopen the Chepstow

service in 1964 but proved tricky to handle in the narrow confines of the Wye. She also made calls at Watchet. Another duty was acting as tender to the Swedish-America Line's cruise ships at Llandudno and she was involved in an awkward incident there in May of 1969: while going alongside the liner *Kungsholm*, her screws were fouled by a towline, she became unmanageable, and hundreds of American tourists spent an uncomfortable night adrift in Llandudno Bay until taken off by the Llandudno lifeboat. The declining trade on the North Wales coast, and the fact that *St Trillo* was really too small for Bristol Channel operations, forced her withdrawal for the 1970 season, and she was laid up at Barry in October 1969. She was offered for sale at a price of £15,000 but no buyer had been found by August 1972.

76 St Trillo *in the Bristol Channel, 4 May 1964*

VECTA/WESTWARD HO (II)

Type	Steel Twin-screw Motor Vessel
GRT	630 tons
Length	199.5ft
Breadth	30.2ft
Depth	8.7ft
Builders	J. I. Thornycroft & Co, Southampton
Engine Makers	English Electric Co
Engine Type	2 SCSA 6 cyls, 380 x 510mm
Yard No	1,180
Speed	15.5 knots

The second motor vessel to enter the White Funnel Fleet arrived in the Bristol Channel in September 1965 on charter from the Southampton, Isle of Wight & South of England Royal Mail Steam Packet Company Ltd—

77 Westward Ho (II) *in 1970 off Clevedon Pier*

better known as the Red Funnel Line. That company had built her in 1938 for the Cowes-Southampton ferry, and she was launched on 14 July of that year. The Hon Mrs Pleydell-Bouverie named her *Vecta*, the Roman name for the Isle of Wight. She caused something of a sensation in shipping circles, as she had Voith-Schneider propulsion, a novelty in those days. In fact, the late delivery of the machinery from Germany prevented her entering service until April 1939. Following the war, and the destruction of German industry, spares were difficult to obtain and she was converted to twin-screw electric drive in 1946. Besides the routine ferry work to Cowes, on which she carried twenty motor cars, *Vecta* also made excursions to the Isle of Wight resorts, and occasionally ran the round-the-Island trip.

Vecta arrived in the Bristol Channel on 21 September 1965, and one of her earliest jobs in her new role was a charter to carry the Bristol City Council on an inspection of Avon-

mouth Docks. Bought by Campbell's parent firm Townsend Car Ferries, in the winter of 1965-6, she was taken in hand by Cosens' yard at Weymouth, where her car deck was covered and converted into passenger saloon accommodation, which increased her tonnage to 739 gross. She was renamed *Westward Ho*. She started operations in the Bristol Channel for the 1966 season, and remained there, usually carrying out the Upper Bristol Channel work, together with the Cardiff-Weston ferry. Her slow speed sometimes made the Ilfracombe run something of an endurance test!

At the end of the 1971 season she suffered an increasing number of mechanical breakdowns and an announcement of her withdrawal for the rest of the season was made on 14 September. She was laid up at Barry with *St Trillo*, and at that time her emergence for the 1972 season looked doubtful indeed. These doubts were confirmed when she later limped on one engine to Hayle in Cornwall, where she was laid up and offered for sale. In October 1972 she was bought for use as a floating restaurant at Manchester by Compass Caterers Ltd and towed to the Mersey.

QUEEN OF THE ISLES

Type	Twin-screw Motor Vessel, Steel-built
GRT	515 tons
Length	142.5ft
Breadth	29.0ft
Depth	13.0ft
Builders	Charles Hill & Sons Ltd, Albion Dockyard, Bristol
Engine Makers	Ruston & Hornsby Ltd
Engine Type	Two 6 cyl diesels, 8 x 10.75in
Shaft HP	573 each
Yard No	448
Speed	13.5 knots

Campbell's made use of this motor vessel during 1968, 1969 and 1970. She was chartered from the Isles of Scilly Steam Ship Company, which had ordered her in 1964 as a relief ship on their Penzance/St Mary's service. The trade to the Scilly Isles never really justified the building of the ship, and she spent much time on day trips round Land's End and was often on charter. Campbell's probably used her more in her latter years than did her owners.

Queen of the Isles was launched on 16 November 1964 at Bristol and named by HRH the Duchess of Gloucester. She was somewhat stubby in appearance, probably because she was designed for future lengthening. Her first trip for Campbell's was the Isles of Scilly three-day excursion in May 1968, and she also ran services for the company in North Wales, calling at such places as Menai Bridge, Llandudno, Liverpool and Douglas, Isle of Man. Following this, *Queen of the Isles* made a so-called 'proving' trip from Cardiff to Dover, calling at Ilfracombe, Penzance, Weymouth, Bournemouth, Eastbourne and Hastings.

The 1969 season found *Queen of the Isles* chartered by Campbell's again and employed in excursions from Hastings and Eastbourne. She operated to the Isle of Wight, and at alternate weekends went round to the Thames overnight to operate from Tower Pier to Southend and Margate on Saturdays and from Southend to Calais on Sundays. She also visited Ostend. The 1969 season was the last that the company operated on the south coast with White Funnel ships, however, and they did not employ *Queen of the Isles* in 1970 except for one tendering charter. The ship did some excursions for private operators from Torquay to Guernsey on 29 and 31 August 1970, when it had already been announced

78 Queen of the Isles *during her English Channel season in 1969*

that she had been sold to the Tongan Government for service in the South Pacific. The price was £153,000 and she sailed from Penzance on 2 December 1970 for Tonga via the Azores, Panama Canal and Tahiti. She is now named *Olovaha* and is used on the inter-island service of the Tonga Shipping Agency.

79 Balmoral *in Cumberland Basin, Bristol, at the start of a charity cruise*

BALMORAL	
Type	Twin-screw Steel Motor Vessel
GRT	688
Length	203.5ft
Breadth	32.0ft
Depth	8.9ft
Builders	J. I. Thornycroft & Co Ltd, Southampton
Engine Makers	Builders
Engine Type	2 SCSA
	2 x 6 cyl, $12\frac{5}{8}$ x $16\frac{3}{4}$in
NHP	600 ea (1,200 total)
Yard No	4120
Speed	15 knots

Business in the Bristol Channel took an upswing when Campbell's chartered this handy little motor vessel from the Southampton company at the beginning of the 1969 season. She joined *Westward Ho*, and soon proved to be as fast as the *Bristol Queen* on some routes, although her performance in heavy weather left a lot to be desired. Two steamers of the same type and operating potential allowed more comprehensive sailings, particularly in the lower Channel, and neglected ports like Bideford, Tenby, Porthcawl, Watchet and Minehead were once again visited. The charter continued for the 1970 and 1971 seasons, *Balmoral* usually operating on the Swansea-Ilfracombe-Lundy services, though she also performed some society charters early in the season, such as a trip round the Isle of Wight and an excursion from Liverpool to Llandudno and Menai Bridge. This latter was in connection with a visit north to tender the cruise liner *Kungsholm*.

80 Balmoral *landing passengers at Lundy in October 1971. The company keeps a fleet of motor launches at Lundy, as it used to at other pier-less resorts, such as Lynmouth and Clovelly*

The Red Funnel Line ordered *Balmoral* in the autumn of 1947. She was launched on 27 June 1949 by Mrs Lena Pinnock and delivered at the end of that year. *Balmoral* was designed for the Southampton-Cowes all-the-year-round service and could carry about twelve cars aft. In latter years the ship was employed most frequently on Solent cruises and excursions round the Isle of Wight, but was withdrawn in the autumn of 1968. The charter to P. & A. Campbell followed.

The announcement by that company on 14 September 1971 that they were withdrawing from the Upper Bristol Channel services, other than charter work, could mean that *Balmoral* will be the last vessel to operate in Campbell colours.

OTHER BRISTOL-BASED SHIPS

Bristol and Ilfracombe Pleasure Steamers Ltd

BRODICK CASTLE

Type	Iron Paddle Steamer
GRT	283
Length	207.6ft
Breadth	21.7ft
Depth	7.5ft
Builders	H. McIntyre, Paisley
Engine Makers	King & Co, Glasgow
Engine Type	2cyl Diagonal, $38\frac{1}{4}$-66in
Reg HP	96
Yard No	19

Brodick Castle operated at Bristol for one season in 1894 under charter from the Bournemouth, Swanage & Poole Steam Packet Co. She appeared at Hotwells with a black hull and upperworks and entered the Ilfracombe trade. It must be assumed that the venture was unsuccessful, as *Brodick Castle* returned to the south coast in 1895. She had been built for the Clyde in 1878 and was brought to Bournemouth 9 years later. Cosens of Weymouth bought her in 1901, but they continued to station her at Bournemouth until 1910, when she was sold off for cattle-carrying. The old ship avoided this indignity by sinking off Portland while on tow to the Argentine.

81 *The old Clyde steamer* Brodick Castle *did a season at Bristol in 1894*

Edwin Hunt

HEATHER BELLE

Type	Iron Paddle Steamer
GRT	271
Length	207.7ft
Breadth	21.0ft
Depth	8.8ft
Builders	Blackwood, Glasgow
Engine Makers	Builders
NHP	200
Yard No	110
Speed	12 knots

This Clyde steamer was 30 years old when Hunt used her for work at Bristol in 1901 and 1902. She came to the Channel after working in railway ownership on the south coast for over two decades, and had already suffered one near miss with breakers. Contemporary photographs show her looking very smart for her age, but she was quite out of her class and the venture ended in 1902. The ship was sold for breaking up.

Hunt tried again in 1905, when he chartered the Lytham-built *Ribble Queen* for one season. She was a twin-screw vessel of less than 100grt, 98ft long. Even on the short trips out of Bristol and Newport for which Hunt employed her she must have been something of a trial in choppy weather, and her stay was short-lived.

82 (*above*) *Edwin Hunt's* Heather Belle *at Bristol*

83 (*below*) *The minute* Ribble Queen *on charter to Hunt in 1905*

CARDIFF-BASED SHIPS

Edwards & Robertson Ltd

Edwards started his Cardiff excursion business in 1883 and acquired the *Lady Margaret* (144 grt, 139.9ft x 18.1ft) in 1884. She was built by Russell & Co at Greenock, and engined by Alley & MacLellan. George Robertson joined Edwards in the business, and *Lady Margaret* ran in their interest over most of the Channel routes between Cardiff, Bristol and Ilfracombe before they sold her to the Medway Steam Packet Co in 1888.

A replacement, again named *Lady Margaret*, was bought in the same year. This was an old Scots steamer named *Carrick Castle* (179 grt, 192ft x 8.9ft), which was built as early as 1870 by Fullerton at Paisley.

In 1889 Edwards & Robertson brought out a new steel paddler, the *Lady Gwendoline*, built for them at Paisley by MacArthur & Co and engined by Bow & MacLachlan. Her tonnage was 427 grt and she was 210.8ft long. With her, the company entered the Bristol service permanently, and she operated there in 1889 and 1890. In the latter year she was advertised as capable of performing the Bristol-Ilfracombe run in less than 4 hours, an optimistic forecast since *Lady Gwendoline* was plagued with boiler trouble. Her owners disposed of her to foreign owners at the end of the 1890 season. *Lady Margaret* (II) and *Lady Gwendoline* appear in Plate 3 (p14).

84 *(below) Edwards' first* Lady Margaret

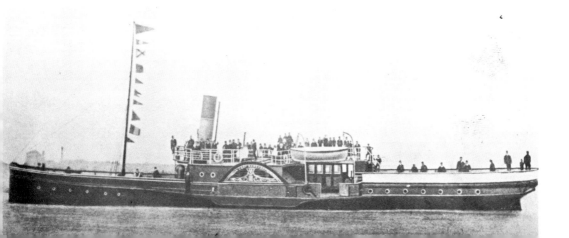

LORNA DOONE

Type	Steel Paddle Steamer
GRT	410
Length	220.5ft
Breadth	26.0ft
Depth	9.2ft
Builders	Napier, Shanks & Bell Ltd
Engine Makers	D. Rowan & Co
Engine Type	Compound diagonal
	2 cyl, 32in, 60-62in
NHP	248
Yard No	54
Speed	16.5 knots

This splendid ship came out in 1891, and is famous for her tussle in the years that followed with White Funnel vessels. She had bad luck right at the start of her Bristol Channel career when, due to an engineering fault, she rammed the tug *Dunrobin* at Ilfracombe and damaged herself. The passengers were brought home by *Ravenswood*, whose owners lost no opportunity in pointing out the Welsh company's discomfiture. *Lorna Doone* remained on the Bristol station until she was sold to John Gunn in 1895, and he in his turn sold her to the Southampton Company in 1898.

In 1899 she was reboiled and appeared with two funnels, but further work led to the removal of the second stack by 1902. *Lorna Doone* remained at Southampton for the rest of her long life, and was a great favourite at that port and at Bournemouth. She served in both World Wars, but at the end of her second naval stint she was not refitted, and was broken up in 1949.

John Gunn

John Gunn also acquired *Bonnie Doon* (p57), *Scotia* (p53) and *Lord Tredegar* (the renamed *Lady Margaret* II) when he bought

85 *The formidable* Lorna Doone, *Cardiff-based challenger of the Campbells in the 1890s*

up the Edwards & Robertson fleet at the end of 1895. When the Gunn fleet was dispersed, *Bonnie Doon* and *Scotia* went to Campbell's and *Lord Tredegar* was scrapped.

W. H. Tucker & Co

In addition to *Lady Evelyn* and *Lady*

SWANSEA-BASED SHIPS

Pockett's Bristol Channel Steam Packet Co Ltd

	VELINDRA
Type	Iron Paddle Steamer
GRT	199
Length	158.4ft
Breadth	19.1ft
Depth	9.1ft
Builders	C. J. Mare, London
Engine Makers	Builders. Re-engined 1888 by Beckwith of Swansea

Velindra, (Plate 17, p33) did not become a full-time excursion steamer until the last years of her long career, which began in 1860 and ended in the breaker's yard in 1897. Her main service to the area was the regular Bristol-Swansea run, and she was a popular favourite at the former port, where a public house still carries her name. Slim in appearance, *Velindra* possessed raked bell-mouthed funnels that looked very attractive. The regular Swansea run ended in 1891, and the ship was thereafter used from Swansea on excursions until broken up at Bristol.

Moyra, Tucker's used the twin-screw steamer *Robina* (306 grt, 156.6ft x 26.1ft) in the Bristol Channel in 1920 and 1921. Built at Ardrossan for the New Morecambe Central Pier Co in 1914, she went on war service and then to Blackpool before being chartered by Tucker's. They attempted winter operations with her but the venture was unsuccessful. The vessel was to have numerous owners, and operated at such diverse places as Belfast, the Western Isles and the Solent before being scrapped in 1953.

	BRIGHTON
Type	Steel Paddle Steamer
GRT	566
Length	221.3ft
Breadth	27.7ft
Depth	10.6ft
Builders	John Elder & Co, Govan
Engine Makers	Builders
Engine Type	Compound diagonal 2 cyl, 48-83in, 60in
NHP	351
Yard No	217
Speed	13.5 knots

Brighton (see also Plate 18, p34) and her sister *Victoria* were built in 1878 for the Newhaven-Dieppe service of the London, Brighton & South Coast Railway. She had the speed so necessary for that service, but had bad luck in her relations with Dieppe pier, which she rammed on her maiden voyage. This pier also ended her railway career, in 1893 when she collided with it and sank just inside the entrance.

Raised and repaired, *Brighton* thereafter ran successfully for Pockett's on the Swansea station, although her trial run after repairs at Bristol produced one of the few fatal accidents ever to occur to a Bristol Channel pleasure steamer. She ran aground at the Horseshoe Bend of the Avon while outward bound in an attempt to avoid the incoming *Lorna Doone*, and in the subsequent panic a number of the passengers jumped overboard, one of them being fatally injured on the rocks below.

Brighton was sold to Turkish owners in 1919 after war service.

86 Brighton *arrives at Ilfracombe. She had the lines of a typical late Victorian railway steamer*

MAVIS	
Type	Steel Paddle Steamer
GRT	474
Length	210.3ft
Breadth	26.3ft
Width	9.4ft
Builders	J. Scott & Co, Kinghorn
Engine Makers	Builders
Engine Type	Compound diagonal 2 cyl, 33in, 61-60in
NHP	240
Yard No	59
Speed	14.5 knots

Mavis was one of five very similar 17-knot vessels built between 1887 and 1889 for the Thames and East coast services of the General Steam Navigation Company. They came out with one funnel forward of the bridge and two masts, but the mainmast was later removed. All five served without incident and were sold off the Thames between 1904 and 1912, *Mavis* coming to the Bristol Channel in 1910. Pockett's retained her ornithological name, and used her until 1913, when she was laid up. She was eventually sold for scrapping in 1915.

87 Mavis *at Bristol in 1911. She was one of four sister ships built for Thames estuary excursions*

James Jones & Company

Jones ran two paddlers from Swansea between 1891 and 1896, both of which carried the name *Alexandra*. The first was an old railway steamer built as long ago as 1863 by Caird of Greenock for the London, Brighton & South Coast Railway. The LB & SC sold her in 1883, and she ran under several flags until she came on to the Swansea-Milford services in 1891. Jones sold her to South Coast owners in 1894, and replaced her with an even older ship—*Aquila* of 1854.

Built for the North Sea at Renfrew, she eventually served the Channel Islands from Weymouth and then passed through the hands of several owners before Jones used her in 1895 and 1896. He renamed her *Alexandra*. Her clipper bow and two thin funnels made an unusual contrast to the modern saloon steamers as Plate 7 shows (p20). Jones sold her off the Channel in 1897, and she was broken up in 1899, after a further change of name.

88 Alexandra *(1863) after her rebuild by James Jones*

J. R. Richards

Yet another London, Brighton & South Coast Railway steamer appeared at Swansea in 1903—the steel paddler *Normandy* (605 grt, 231ft long), built by Elder at Glasgow in 1882. After 20 years in the English Channel, a private operator tried her out against the Isle of Man Steam Packet Co's service between Liverpool and Douglas, with the inevitable result. Hence she came to Swansea in 1903. She ran five seasons against the *Brighton* to Ilfracombe, and went to the breakers in 1909.

W. K. David

In 1920 the former North British Railway steamer *Lady Rowena* sailed out of Swansea for a brief season under the ownership of W. K. David. Built by McKnight of Ayr in 1891 and 332 grt, she had been in Italy, Newhaven, Belfast and the Humber, as well as acting as a minesweeper, before coming to South Wales. She had lost her Clyde livery and 'looks' by this time and had a difficult season, after which she was laid up. She was sold again, and eventually scrapped in 1923.

89 Lady Rowena *in North British colours on the Clyde*

APPENDIX 1:
BIOGRAPHICAL SKETCHES

CAPTAIN PETER CAMPBELL

Captain Peter Campbell was born on 14 December 1858 at Row in Dumbartonshire, the elder son of Captain and Mrs Robert Campbell. He was educated at Glasgow Academy and served an engineering apprenticeship with Messrs W. King & Company at their Glasgow engineering works. He joined King's in 1881 and early in his career served in the merchant vessel *Strathleven*, which was the first refrigerated ship to bring meat in bulk from Australia.

He returned to Glasgow in the mid-1880s and joined his father's fleet of excursion steamers. At this time he studied navigation, and was one of the first men to possess both Master Mariner's and Chief Engineer's certificates. He remained on the Clyde until 1891, when he came south to Bristol to take over command of *Waverley*. As the White Funnel Fleet expanded, Captain Peter became Commodore of the fleet and also Engineering Director. The company usually carried out all its own repairs, and from 1917 onwards Captain Peter presided at the Underfall Repair Yard in Bristol's Floating Harbour.

Throughout these years he lived at 19 Oakfield Road, Clifton. As a young man he was a keen rugby player, and later became a good shot.

On the death of his younger brother in 1928 Captain Peter became joint Managing Director of the company, from which he retired in 1936, going to live at Wootton-under-Edge. He died on 18 December 1938, four days after his eightieth birthday. Mrs Peter Campbell had died in 1937, and the couple left two sons and a daughter. Captain Campbell is buried at Wootton-under-Edge.

90 *Captain Peter Campbell* 91 *Captain Alec Campbell*

CAPTAIN ALEXANDER CAMPBELL

Captain Alexander Campbell was born in 1863 and was the younger son of Captain Robert Campbell. His early career is not so well recorded as that of his elder brother, but it seems that, following education at Glasgow Academy, he went to sea as an apprentice with his father in the Clyde steamboats.

One writer has said that Alec Campbell was educated on the bridge of a paddle steamer, and this is probably true. Certainly he inherited from his father a flair for operating these lovely vessels at the limit of their performance, and he won an early reputation for enterprising seamanship. It was due to his drive in the early days at Bristol that the White Funnel Fleet became the commercial success that it was.

Captain Alec was no stranger to litigation. He survived a Board of Trade Inquiry in 1893, led the fight in the courts against the Barry Railway Company in 1907 and was again in court in 1909 following serious injuries he sustained in an accident with a taxi cab. On this last occasion he was awarded heavy damages.

In the early twentieth century Alec Campbell was one of Bristol's best known citizens, and in 1910 he became President of the Bristol Caledonian Society. During all this time he acted as Managing Director of the company and lived in the city, but in 1914 he married Miss Ethel West of Redland and thereafter lived at Kilmun. He travelled to Bristol each March for the opening of the paddle-boat excursion season.

In his latter years Captain Alec Campbell suffered from heart trouble and he died at his home at Ferngrove, Kilmun, on 10 December 1928 at the age of sixty-five.

92 (above) White Funnel noon. A bright day on Britannia in the 1950s

93 (above right) White Funnel splendour. Glen Gower celebrates a Royal Visit to Bristol in 1956

94 (centre right) White Funnel morning. An excursion party on Bristol Queen pauses for the camera

95 (right) White Funnel midnight. Bristol Queen rests from her labours in Bristol's Cumberland Basin

APPENDIX 2: FARES FROM BRISTOL

The following table shows typical Channel return fares charged in 1898 and those for 1971, which was the last season that pleasure steamers operated from Bristol:

Bristol to:	1898		1971
	Foredeck	Saloon	£
WESTON	1/6	2/-	.80
PORTISHEAD	1/-	1/-	.30
CARDIFF	2/-	2/6	.90
BARRY	2/-	2/6	1.20
ILFRACOMBE	3/-	5/-	2.00
MUMBLES	3/-	5/-	2.00
Children	Half Price (Under 12)		Half Price (Under 14)
Dogs	1/- each way		25p return
Bicycles	1/- each way		50p each way

BIBLIOGRAPHY

BOOKS

Burtt, Frank. *Cross Channel and Coastal Paddle Steamers* (Tilling 1934)

— *Steamers of the Thames & Medway* (Tilling 1949)

Duckworth & Langmuir. *Clyde River & Other Steamers*, revised ed (Glasgow: Brown Son & Ferguson 1972)

— *Railway & Other Steamers*, 2nd ed (Prescot: Stephenson 1968)

— *West Coast Steamers*, revised ed (Prescot: Stephenson 1965)

— *West Highland Steamers*, 3rd ed (Prescot: Stephenson 1967)

Farr, Grahame E. *West Country Steamers*, 2nd ed (Prescot: Stephenson 1967)

Grasemann & McLachlan. *English Channel Packet Boats* (Syren & Shipping 1939)

Grimshaw, Geoffrey. *British Pleasure Steamers 1920-1939* (Tilling 1945)

Patterson, A. J. S. *The Golden Years of the Clyde Steamers 1889-1914* (Newton Abbot: David & Charles 1969)

— *The Victorian Summer of the Clyde Steamers 1864-1888* (Newton Abbot: David & Charles 1972)

Thornley, F. C. *Steamers of North Wales* (Prescot: Stephenson 1952)

Thornton, E. C. B. *South Coast Pleasure Steamers*, 2nd ed (Prescot: Stephenson 1969)

— *Thames Coast Pleasure Steamers* (Prescot: Stephenson 1972)

Warne, F. G. *Bristol Channel Guide*, various eds (Bristol: P. & A. Campbell)

MAGAZINES AND PERIODICALS

Cruising Monthly—Journal of Coast Cruising Association

Harbour Light—Swansea Branch of the World Ship Society

Lloyd's Register of Shipping

Marine News—Journal of the World Ship Society

Model Boats

Paddle Wheels—The Journal of the Paddle Steamer Preservation Society

Sea Breezes

Ship Ahoy—South Wales Branch of World Ship Society

Shipbuilder, The

Ships and Ship Models

Ships Monthly

NEWSPAPERS

Bournemouth Echo

Bristol Evening Post

Bristol Evening World

Bristol Times and Mirror

Lloyd's List

Times, The

Western Daily Press

Western Mail

COLLECTIONS

Photographic Collection of Ilfracombe Museum

York Collection and Catalogue—Bristol City Museum

ACKNOWLEDGEMENTS

Many people have helped in the work of producing this book, and I acknowledge particularly the help of S. C. Smith-Cox, Chairman and Managing Director of P. & A. Campbell Ltd; the Cultural Committee of Bristol Corporation, and in particular the Director of the City Museum, Nicholas Thomas, his predecessor, Alan Warhurst, and Paul Elkin, Technical Curator at the Museum; my fellow members of the Port of Bristol Authority; George Edney, General Manager of the Port of Bristol, and his deputy, Gordon Lowery; the Ministry of Defence (Navy); the City Public Relations Officer of Bristol, J. Lavery Crook, and his deputy, R. Sawyer; the British Transport Docks Board; Upper Clyde Shipbuilders Ltd; Red Funnel Steamers Ltd; the General Steam Navigation Co Ltd; the Imperial War Museum; Captain H. Rawnsley of Ilfracombe Museum; Peter Lamb, Curator of the Paddle Steamer Preservation Society; F. R. Sherlock of the World Ship Society; Patrick Murrell; Michael Cassar; and A. Taylor.

Ernest Dumbleton has provided photographs from his extensive collection. His knowledge of the pleasure steamers is almost encyclopaedic, and I am grateful for his help and friendship. Gordon Farnsworth, Editor of the *Bristol Evening Post*, and Eric Price, Editor of the *Western Daily Press*, and their staffs have given me much useful and pointed advice, and the staff of the Reference Library at Bristol have helped in finding many early newspapers and publications. Miss Margaret Dickason (now Mrs Kevin Doore) and Miss Christine Yandell typed the manuscript and suffered many alterations to it with much forbearance.

I am also grateful to the following for permission to use photographs in their possession: Bristol Corporation City Museum, York Collection, for 2, 18, 19, 20, 25, 27, 32, 33, 37, 38, 40, 41, 44, 48, 52, 56, 82, 83, 87; *Bristol Evening Post* for 23, 36, 58, 71, 76, 79; P. & A. Campbell Ltd for 22, 30, 46, 61, 68; Michael Cassar for 74; Ernest Dumbleton for 35, 59, 64, 94; Ernest Dumbleton Collection for 1, 6, 9, 10, 11, 21, 24, 26, 28, 29, 34, 39, 43, 50, 51, 54, 60, 63, 85, 88, 90, 91; British Transport Docks Board for 14; Ilfracombe Museum for 3, 5, 7, 17, 86; Patrick Murrell for 57, 70, 73, 75, 95; Port of Bristol Authority for 4, 12, 13, 15, 16, 53, 92, 93; Ministry of Defence (Navy) for 31a, 55a, 61a, 69; Paddle Steamer Preservation Society for 31, 49, 55, 62; Skyfotos Ltd for 78; Upper Clyde Shipbuilders Ltd for 8, 42, 45, 47, 65, 72; and World Ship Society for 66, 67, 81. Nos 77, 80, 84 and 89 come from my own collection.

Finally, I must record my thanks to my wife for her encouragement and advice, without which this book would not have been written.

ROBERT WALL

Bristol, 1972.

GENERAL INDEX

Italic figures indicate pages with illustrations

INDEX OF SHIPS

Italic figures indicate pages with illustrations